Making High Profits in Uncertain Times

Successful Investing in
Inflation and Depression

Making High Profits in Uncertain Times

Successful Investing in Inflation and Depression

Robert M. Barnes

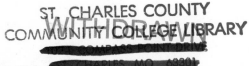

VAN NOSTRAND REINHOLD COMPANY
NEW YORK CINCINNATI TORONTO LONDON MELBOURNE

Copyright © 1982 by Van Nostrand Reinhold Company Inc.

Library of Congress Catalog Card Number: 82-2006
ISBN: 0-442-21299-2

Manufactured in the United States of America

Published by Van Nostrand Reinhold Company Inc.
135 West 50th Street, New York, N.Y. 10020

Van Nostrand Reinhold Publishing
1410 Birchmount Road
Scarborough, Ontario MIP 2E7, Canada

Van Nostrand Reinhold Australia Pty. Ltd.
17 Queen Street
Mitcham, Victoria 3132, Australia

Van Nostrand Reinhold Company Limited
Molly Millars Lane
Wokingham, Berkshire, England

15 14 13 12 11 10 9 8 7 6 5 4 3 2 1

Library of Congress Cataloging in Publication Data

Barnes, Robert M.
    Making high profits in uncertain times.

    Includes index.
    1. Commodity exchanges.   I. Title.
HG6046.B337   332.63'28   82-2006
ISBN 0-442-21299-2   AACR2

Introduction

The investment world is in great turmoil. Traditionally safe areas like bonds or conservative stocks like AT&T not only do not pay dividends to keep up with inflation but are in *real danger* of losing considerable market value. Will the stock market ever recover again? Even real estate is no sure winner anymore: can values keep pace with rising costs, and can one ever be sure of selling the property? Nothing is sure, and nothing seems to keep pace with inflation, the arch enemy. The profits in our portfolios become smaller and fewer in number as the period of easy investment winnings comes to an end.

Commodities are one of the very few investment exceptions. While inflation has averaged about ten percent over the past twenty years, commodities have performed as a group *twice as well*, gaining nearly twenty percent a year on average! This means the average commodity investment has gained ten percent a year *after* inflation. Because commodity futures are leveraged investments they are risky, and many people do lose money trading this vehicle.

But investors don't have to lose in commodities. With the right plan, enough capital, and patience, the average person can be a *big* winner in this fast-paced area. Return on capital of hundreds, even thousands, of percent a year are entirely possible. The profit opportunities are there (see chapters on gold, sugar, T-bills in the past two years, to name a very few of the many examples). It is quite possible to attain ten-, fifty-, and even a hundred-fold increases on the commodity margin (capital) invested, in a short period of time.

An efficient money-making plan to time trades, minimize losses, maximize gains, catch the major trends, and identify large profit potential is needed. The one discussed in this book can be utilized easily, and has been tested in history for efficacy. The plan leaves virtually no room for guess work or judgment on the part of the investor, as it is mechanical, but also requires no advanced mathematical skills to operate.

The book is divided into essentially five sections. The first discusses the history, reason for, and effects of the huge inflationary period on the public and the investor in particular, now and in the near future (Chapter 1). The broad panorama of investments in general and commodities in special detail are examined in the light of the looming investment doom (Chapter 2).

The third section, Chapter 3, delves into commodities in greater detail. The history, mechanics, monies involved, profit potential, reason for existence, facts and figures, what is traded, opening an account, types of orders, statements, and tax considerations are spelled out.

The management plan to make money in commodities is presented in Chapter 4, the fourth section. The Profit Finder, the device to select the best commodity for maximum profit, is detailed, and examples given. A second tool, the Profit Timer, is set forth. This allows the investor to determine when to best time his purchases and sales of each commodity under study. How is it used, examples, and simple calculation procedures are explained.

The Management Plan puts these two tools together for a complete, optimum methodology. One option allows the reader to choose and concentrate on those special few commodities he feels strongly will outperform all other commodities. The other option is for those desiring a completely automatic plan, one that tells him what commodities to include in his portfolio, when to include them, when to buy and sell, how much of each to have included, and what to expect in returns in the long run. The second option is set up to be the investor's own personal "mutual fund" in commodities, with smooth, long-term, way-above-average profits as the objective.

Chapter 5 explains how to easily read the profit results table found in each of the commodity chapters. It is these tables that will indicate the great potential profits available to the reader.

Chapter 6 through 22 comprise the fifth section, and cover commodities and their profit potentials from A to Z, cattle to wheat. Each chapter gives an overview on a commodity. Second, each commodity's profit potential (quite large in most cases) during the past twenty years (or its life, if it is a young commodity) is discussed. The fundamental characteristics governing the commodity (supply, demand, growing conditions, politics, etc.) follows. Important events and their effects tell the investor what happenings can make prices explode. The Profit Timer method's trade results are all-important and indicate to the reader how he will make profits (and how much) during big boom and bust periods and how the Timer will behave during lull times. A peek into the future completes the survey of each commodity.

Contents

Introduction v

1. Catastrophic Inflation and Depression Are Coming 1
2. How Different Investments Will Fare 13
3. Commodities, From A to Z 20
4. The Plan to Make Money 51
5. Trading Results Explained 71
6. Cattle Profits 74
7. Cocoa Profits 80
8. Coffee Profits 85
9. Copper Profits 90
10. Corn Profits 95
11. Cotton Profits 100
12. Profits in the Currencies 105
13. Profits in the Financial Instruments 119
14. Gold Profits 129
15. Hog Profits 134
16. Lumber Profits 139
17. Orange Juice Profits 144
18. Pork Belly Profits 149
19. Silver Profits 154
20. Profits In the Soybean Complex 159
21. Sugar Profits 168
22. Wheat Profits 173

Additional Readings 179
Index 181

1.
Catastrophic Inflation and Depression are Coming

We had glimpses of it in 1974 and 1980: twelve percent prime rate, soaring food costs, and the beginning of inflation as we have not known in our lifetimes.

The first wave receded for six years and seemed like a momentary nightmare. With increased intensity, however, the wave returned in 1980. Long gas lines were a precursor of what was to come: interest rates unbelievably in the mid-twenties, sharp inflation in the high teens, and almost permanent death to huge segments of our economy: the bond, auto, and housing markets.

It is no longer a passing nightmare. The second wave in 1980 let us know it is no fluke. Inflation, its cruel effects and aftermath, is here to stay. There may be momentary lulls, enough to fool many people to forget about the economic scourge, but it will always return, stronger and more horrible.

What will it be like to live with inflation and its effects? Will there be momentary lulls, or weird aftermaths, like the shock waves and successive smaller, but more rapid, tremors following major earthquakes?

What are the causes of this ogre?

Can it be stopped by the government or the private sector?

What will happen to most people? Is there strong evidence to bear out our fears?

To see that indeed a large depression is coming, you should look at some "pictures" of past times, to see that it has occurred and can occur again. Most important, one should grasp that it will occur even stronger next time.

EVIDENCE OF THE COMING CATASTROPHY

General prices, as measured by the wholesale price index (it could be any other similar measure), have steadily and dramatically soared over the past ten years, while wages, stock values, and other income measures have crept up slowly. Figure 1 depicts stock price movements and the wholesale price index (WPI) on the same chart. Stock prices (Dow Jones Industrial Average, not the best but a representative one) generally vacillated between 600 and 1,000 (right scale) over the past twenty years. The WPI, on the other hand, steadily rose from 95 (left scale) to about 270 by 1981, almost a 200% increase! And the past ten years accounted for the greatest part of it — an enormous, streaking move amounting to about 15% per year!

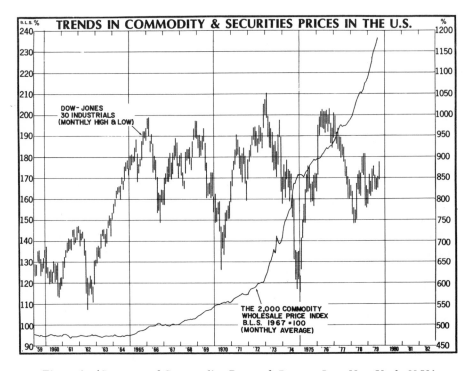

Figure 1. (Courtesy of Commodity Research Bureau, Inc., New York, N.Y.)

Did your wages or income increase that much per year, every year, in the past ten years? The difference between 15% and your actual wage increase means the *loss* in standard of living — how much less you can buy now for your hard-earned money.

The American dollar has depreciated nearly 75% in the past 25 years, meaning less purchasing again for your hard-earned dollar. Where will it stop? Is this just a temporary swing against the dollar and against wage increases and purchasing power? Will the nightmare pass away with time? Can we blame all this on free-spending governments?

The dollar may recover at times, especially with respect to European currencies, governments may cut down the increases in public spending and even balance the budget, but the tide toward a lower standard of living is inexorably coming in, to stay.

Is there evidence of this in "bigger pictures," long-term charts? Look at Figure 2. It depicts two series of data-business production, a good indicator of our basic economic health *before* price rise adjustment, or inflation, and wholesale prices, again. The period covered was from 1790 to the present. The first obvious thing to notice is that business production oscillates from good growth times (prosperity) to poor times (depression). Many events and years are identified with these cycles. There are four conclusions about depression we can draw from this chart.

THE FOUR DEPRESSION RELATIONSHIPS

We all tend to look at the prosperity since World War II and think, "Isn't it great?." No, it isn't great for us *now*. Careful scrutiny might tell us that for every boom period there is a bust time lurking just around the corner. And, indeed, if you check over the long history, you will see that the major boom periods were followed by as big and sometimes even bigger bust periods. For instance, maritime commerce prosperity (1805) was quickly followed by an embargo depression (1808). The bank credit land boom was just as quickly followed by the panic of 1837. And so on.

Another relationship also seems to hold: the bigger and/or longer the prosperity period, the bigger and/or longer the following bust times. The prosperity during World War I led to four years of good production, then a primary postwar depression that didn't last long, but it was deep. The ensuing prosperity, until 1929, and its aftermath, the Great Depression, is legend and the biggest on record.

Also, wars beget prosperous times either concurrent to the war or immediately afterwards, and produce not only one depression periods, but two (like secondary tremors after the main earthquake): note the War of 1812, Civil War, World War I — they all preceded two major depressions!

Finally, huge depressions are associated with abnormal rises in wholesale prices. Although there were many depressions (and some were deep) before the Civil War, none lasted more than one or two years. Wholesale prices rose 50% above its long-term trend line as the Civil War ended, and two major depressions followed within ten years, one lasting for nearly six years. Wholesale prices again rose to about 70% above its long-term growth line in 1920, and ten years later the Great Depression began.

The current period completely dwarfs the wholesale rise of 1920. Current prices are nearly *four hundred percent* above the growth line compared to only 70 percent above in 1920, prior to the great depression! God help us if there is a correlation between the magnitude of wholesale price rises and the size of the coming depression!

Indeed, we are well overdue. Production has continued above its growth line, and prices have soared even more, over an unbroken span of forty years.

Summarizing, these facts seem evident and ominous:

1. Every prosperity time has a bust time after it.
2. The bigger the prosperity, the bigger the following bust.
3. War periods produce concurrent or subsequent prosperous times, then two depressions.
4. Abnormal jumps in wholesale prices beget abnormally large depressions (and the larger the price rise, the larger and longer the depression).

Horribly, every one of those conditions fits the current circumstances:

1. We have had uninterrupted prosperity since World War II, but have not had a bust yet.
2. The bust, when it comes, will be large, in keeping with the great prosperity.
3. Our largest war involvement (in terms of total dollars, effort and manpower), World War II, has not seen a subsequent depression, let alone two of them.
4. The abnormal jump in prices to over 400% of the average has yet to cause an equally abnormally large depression.

CAUSES OF SUPER INFLATION

There are many reasons such catastrophies could come about. Douglas Casey, in *Crisis Investing* (1), sees three factors heavily contributing to heated inflation: excesses in our government, private industries, and certain financial structural weaknesses that can bring about an excessive depression.

Casey points out that government spending is in itself probably the main ingredient for rising pressure on prices. It makes up one-third of the gross national product. Government debt is equal to one-half of all the debt in this country, and taxes are five hundred times greater than they were in 1910!

This last fact is rather stupefying. Taxes are one of the most inflationary items around, I believe, because they are spent, whereas nontaxed citizen and corporate funds are mostly saved or reinvested, causing less demand pressure on available funds; hence, lower prices and interest rates.

Ironically, with all the posturing by both the Republican and Democratic administrations about reducing interest rates and inflation, they are the main culprits in spending, which is inflation fuel.

The federal deficit is expanding by a factor of 2.8 times per year, a monstrous rate that calls out for more and more debt monies to be financed through public autions, increasing demand for funds, thus putting upward pressure on interest rates. The money supply continues to stay large, in great part due to growing government money needs. Short-term and even long-term government needs are largely fixed and built into law, so little can be done.

The most any administration can do is to slow down the rate of deficit increase, and keep government money demands on a steady but not reduced course. The tide is not reversible because many programs (social security, defense, certain state aid, and many others) are built to continue to grow, and are considered essential to a modern economy. So we are stuck with a monster we must continue to feed or it will eat us up.

Casey also points out thst the natural forces in the business world create cycles: prosperous times followed by bust, over and over again.   Essentially, this is because business expands too much in profitable times; its rate of profit then starts to diminish, cutbacks are instituted, losses start occurring, investment shrinks, and layoffs occur. But then, the down cycle begins to ebb as unprofitable firms go under, good ones have trimmed down, and an upswing develops with renewed customer sales. Businesses have enjoyed prosperity for a long time, and have expanded and pushed prices higher and realized profits for a nearly unbroken period of forty years. A long, deep, down cycle is long overdue.

The appalling horror is that a real crunch could develop quickly. The financial industry, especially banks, are our money lifeblood; they circulate the stuff of investment and daily economic exchange, money.   They are, however, highly vulnerable to certain crises (note the collapses in the great depression). This is because of their leveraged nature. Yes, they may actually be more volatile than such traditionally risky investment areas as options and commodity futures. Except that banks hide behind respectable images and are supposedly protected by an arm of the government, the Federal Reserve.   But this protection is really based on confidence: the knowledge, or hope, that the U.S. government will bail out the system if it gets in trouble. Yes, the government can print money, but that means even more horrendous inflation, of the 1920s German style (you needed a wheelbarrel full of marks to buy simple grocery items at the peak).

The leverage and consequential weakness in the banking system comes from the fact that banks need only a small fraction of their assets as their own to reimburse citizens if withdrawls are needed. This ratio of total assets to bank capital is presently about 15 to 1, set more or less by the Federal Reserve. The larger the ratio, the more the system totters and is vulnerable to a run on the banks.

Or, just as crucial, a "squeeze" on bank assets could develop if interest rates drop too fast. The monies they owe savers at high rates (older CDs, for example) and need to pay out now could overwhelm repayments they receive on lower-rate monies loaned out currently. Like the run on the bank, this could squeeze the banks for immediate funds, which they would have to run to the market place to get, re-sulting in the jerking up of rates, or the banks would have to be bailed out ultimately by the Federal Reserve.

But the Federal Reserve only has a tiny fraction of actual cash reserves: for every four hundred dollars of private bank assets really belonging to you, the public, the Reserve has only one dollar to make good on any default. Apparently, the government is confident only to the extent of backing the private banking sector with a drop in the bucket.

How our money system totters! A small change in confidence, a small run on the bank, so to speak, can make the government run to print more money, thereby contributing to create catastrophic infla-tion with a depression collapse to follow. Then there would be no more demand for worthless paper money, and goods would not be exchanged or produced. Hence, an awesome depression.

THE THREE CENTRAL REASONS
FOR STRONG INFLATION

Casey reveals some of the symptoms and contributing causes of severe inflation. But I believe there are three central reasons for our and the world's quickening inflation and the specter of depression.

First, the U.S. and the developed world are becoming increasingly service-oriented, with less per capita productivity than in the past. This trend will continue as we value services, such as instant ham-burger lunches or recreation weekends, more highly.

All meaningful (tangible) economic growth in the past has been measured on the basis of goods manufactured, or production per capita. Out standard of living is tied to how many material things we can buy, and our wealth individually measured as such.

With less goods produced, the cost of those goods will surely rise when money supply and population increase. Because of the structure of business today, a sharp drop in goods produced could have a devastating effect on employment, well overcoming gains in employment in service industries. Thus, a sharply dropping productivity rate will contribute greatly to bringing about the inflation followed by severe depression.

Secondly, the world is getting smaller, not geographically, but more dependent and closely knit. Many economics are tied into money developments (interest rates) globally, goods are interchanged faster, and a sneeze in one country makes all the rest shout "achoo!" We are more and more influenced by political, social, and economic events around the globe. There are now many more people chasing fewer goods with more money and appetite. The underdeveloped countries cannot keep up with the thirst for oil and other raw materials. The result is higher prices, greater inflation, then severe depression. We are at the mercy of an Angolan uprising, a Polish crisis, with increasing appetites for more goods in all lands and more money circulating from country to country, at ever quickening tempos.

Thirdly, worldwide population has been burgeoning over the past forty years. No wars have stopped, checked, or slowed down the world population growth. Even the miraculous American farmer is hard pressed to feed the world's hungry mouths. Basically, the world population explosion is at the root of the inflation problem. There simply are more people chasing less goods than can be adequately produced. In the past, major wars, famines, and the state of undeveloped countries (poor malnutrition, health, education, etc.) have kept population growth in check. The past forty years have seen an absence of general conflagrations (enough to substantially reduce population) and natural disasters, and a marked increase in the state of undeveloped and underdeveloped countries. I do not advocate creating major wars or disasters, or hammering these countries back to the Stone Age.

Rather, some constructive channeling of surplus population into productive (materialistic) enterprises must take place, and fast. Superelevated education and training programs should be undertaken.

These three causes — ever-increasing service-oriented economies, an evermore interdependent world economy, and a burgeoning population rate — have all combined to make more money chase fewer goods. The result is superinflation followed by the natural swing in the business cycle to severe depression.

THE FORMS OF DEPRESSION

There have been two types of crashs in modern society, hyperinflation and depression. The first comes about when there is too much in circulation. The paper it's printed on becomes worthless. Economic shock and instability follow, usually with political instability shortly on its heels. The new government then strongly controls the economy in a dictatorial manner, and stability returns — at an unbearable cost. The obvious example of this is the German superheated inflation of the 1920s, the collapse of the Weimar Republic, the takeover by Hitler, and worldwide suffering and loss in World War II. What a way to solve an economic problem.

The second kind is characterized as a severe deflationary reaction to high inflation. The business bubble bursts, a financial crash (loss of value) ensues, stock, bond, and real estate prices come down sharply, unemployment soars, a lack of demand for products takes place, and a general realignment and readjustment of wealth takes place. Our depression of 1929 is the sure example of this type.

Which of these two catastrophies will occur?

Oddly, a combination of the two will probably happen.

We are already in the final phase — the quickening tempo of inflation leading to a soaring rate of hyperinflation.

We are not a shaky political economy. We have lasted through many disasters and economic malaises before, and have kept our way of governing intact and even strengthened it. Indeed, the two prior superinflationary periods have led to depressions, not radical political changes, and brighter times have thereafter ensued. No doubt about it, our form of government will keep us from utter chaos. But it will be a hell-hole depression: long and deep.

There are only two essential ways a government can manipulate the economy. In the first, the administration can keep interest rates high by continuing to restrict money supply.

The net effect is continued inflation and steady loss of standard of living.   In this scenario we will sharply lose our purchasing power.

The second way is to "let it all hang out," or let the business cycle do its natural thing and go into a deep depression, as in the Great Depression, only worse.

No political entity wants that, so governments are reduced to plying a middle course, letting interest rates go down slowly by controlling money supply and cutting government spending and hoping for a slowdown in inflation to a tolerable level while keeping unemployment and other ogres relatively low.   All this does is slow down the inevitable standard-of-living decline and make unemployment a burden.

AN INFLATION-DEPRESSION SCENARIO

What will it be like in the near future?   During the final phase? Whether administrations let events take their course or take the middle course outlined above (which seems more likely — they will try to fool people slowly or gamble that the narrow, tottering course somehow will cool inflation enough to a tolerable level), we face the slow but bottomless trap of sure erosion of living standards.

At first, inflation will hit us to the extent of losing an average of 5% of purchasing power a year, then quickening to 10–15%, and probably reaching a height of 30% before severe depression hits.

This means an average car will cost $20,000 in today's dollars early on, then $100,000 near the peak (the cost of a Rolls-Royce now).   Ironically, citizens of undeveloped and communist countries today face this prospect — they need many years' savings to get what we now consider a staple or necessary item, the car.   However, at the height of roaring inflation (which may reach the high double digits — 50% — and even possibly 100% per year, like Brazil and Israel now), the car will be a highly envied luxury item.   Public transportation will be in heavy use.

Food costs will even soar.   Ten dollars for a loaf of bread may not be unheard of, and jewelry will be rare and socially unacceptable to flash in public.   Somehow, TV and its descendants will remain relative bargains, as if one tiny lifeblood stream will be kept flowing to keep us alive.   Most property will be rented from public housing authorities, and an adventurous vacation will consist of city-to-city travel, with a few lucky lottery winners taking a trip abroad.

Clothes will still be relatively cheap because of plastics and other synthetics.   Many "services" which we take for granted now will be extremely expensive or rare.   Libraries will be jam-packed and books hard to get because retail costs will be $100 and up.   Hamburger palaces will be the Saturday night dinner and evening entertainment (TVs and disks will be an extra while you dine).   Growing one's own vegetables and plants will be a necessity, like washing machines today, only washing machines will be leased or heavily mortgaged.   Neighborhood nightly visits and relatives sharing common households will be standard.   Talk will still be cheap, so most entertainment will center around groups getting together on weekend nights.   Liquor will be expensive, too, but a necessary evil — bathtub gin and its cousins will return.   Miraculously, new forms of energy will continue to be discovered and the cost of some basic services, electricity and heat, will remain moderately inexpensive, only $300–$400 per month per family.   Some good will come of this hardship, however.   Families and friends will stick closer together, more out of common necessity due to severity, and personal values, codes, and relationships will be strengthened.

IS DEPRESSION AVOIDABLE?

Whichever path it takes — German style superinflation followed by a spectacular crash, or the steady slow erosion by inflation of our standard of living — the result will be the same.   We will be faced with buying very little for our income, and we will be poor.   It cannot be avoided by government action or by private industry because it is the inevitable result of the business cycle and excesses that we are currently burdened with.

YOU CAN STILL PROSPER

As a people, we are saddled to the inflation horse, and must wait for it to run its course and ride through the unfortunate times. But as individuals, we can neutralize and even greatly profit from hard times. There are ways inflation can be an investment arm, even a leverage, to *make* and *multiply* wealth, in addition to preserving monies. The following chapters discuss the investment vehicles and simple tools one can use to gain riches.

2.
How Different Investments will Fare

The rational way to combat severe inflation and later depression is for the investor to seek out investment media that will keep pace with inflation and somehow hold value during depression. As you will see, that is an extremely hard task. I contend, however, that the investor can not only find one to preserve his capital but *multiply* it: to actually make it gain *dramatically* during extreme times by taking advantage of the conditions instead of succumbing to them.

You as an investor have many choices. The investment spectrum is broad and complex. Conditions change. Consider that franchises, certificates of deposit, tax shelters, sophisticated types of futures such as currencies and financials, government lotteries, and gold ownership were not even around thirty years ago.

RAINBOW OF INVESTMENTS

Figure 3 shows the rainbow of investments usually available to the general public investor. On one end are low-risk, low-return areas like government bonds and savings, and on the other extreme are forms of gambling. A government treasury bond has almost no risk (unless we kiss off our government and way of life), but the return is small and fixed: 3% in stable, noninflationary times, and as high as low teens in heated inflation. Sometimes they pay better than higher risk instruments like savings (CDs) or even some stocks, which makes investors go for them in droves (hence the current popularity with money funds, which have Treasury bills as the main feature). Money funds have a different feature: they pay out higher rates than

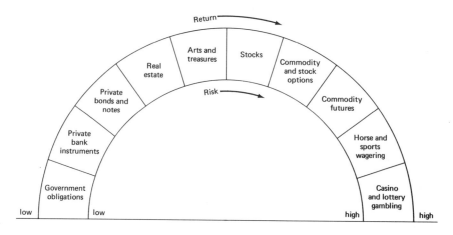

Figure 3. The investment rainbow.

savings most of the time, but vary up and down more than savings. Because of this "varying" feature, they could lose principal if un-balanced liquidation forced management to sell government obliga-tions for losses and consequently are considered more risky than savings. Witness the Salomon Brothers cave-in and takeover because of loss of value of their bond holdings.

Corporate bonds can pay high or low interest rates, and generally fall somewhere in the savings to government range, but can pay more, or less, than either one. An added feature that gives some more capital appreciation potential is the convertible item. If the underlying stock moves up dramatically, the investor can realize a good yield and convert bond shares to stock ownership at a low price, *and* make money on appreciation of the stock.

Real estate often keeps pace with inflation (it's a limited-supply item, "They aint makin' any more of it."), rising as much as twenty percent a year nationwise in surging inflation times, and going side-ways in recessions. But there are maintenance costs, which cut into profits. The potential for gain is uneven: recreation property has been a steady gainer throughout time, but urban property, due to inner-city blight, has gone down in value much of the time.

Art collection has increased both as an enjoyment and profit media. Gambles are taken, however. Works by unknown artists make for uncertain, unknown values — only a very few out of thousands will prove out as famous as Gaugin in value, and maybe only one in thirty has an average appreciation close to inflation. Proven art (masterpieces) kept their value and even increased in the early 1980s, but average art *lost* value and followed recessions simply because the general public stopped buying, because necessities came first before this "luxury."

Coins, particularly older and rarer ones (e.g., Greek and Roman) have held value, increasing between 15–20% per year for the past thirty years. They have two values, the rarity and collection properties, and the basic metal value (gold content). The market place is small and spread out, however, making it hard to quickly and without great price change liquidate the goods. The area is very dependent on steady collectors' interest and the rising price of the coins' metal. Stamps and other collectibles parallel coins and art treasury in that they too can be enjoyed, and their value can go up appreciably, but they too suffer from narrow interest or fads.

Stocks represent a wide range of return and risk. Some conservative stocks (GE) grow slowly but have high yields, while really speculative ones can jump from $1 or $2 per share to $100, with little dividend payments. Influences from the economy, government, industry, and geography can turn the market as a whole or individual stocks in one direction or another. Investor psychology can greatly extend price moves, as in the 1974 and 1980 recessions, which became deep.

Stock and commodity options rank high in return on investment because of the leverage (typically 15–20%) available to investors. For a fixed period of time, a holder of an option can purchase (or sell) a given amount of stock or commodity at a previously agreed upon price. For this right, he pays an amount of money (the premium). If the stock's (commodity's) price prior to the expiration date is considerably better than the agreed upon price and means a large enough profit for him, the investor will exercise the option. Often there is less profit and even none before the period is up, however, which means he loses part or all of his original investment (the premium). Much of the time this is the case.

Commodity futures can be more speculative than options. The trader puts up even less of the value of what he is trading (usually 5–10%, except in extremely volatile times). A change of only 5% or

10% in the price of the commodity could double or triple his stake, or clean it out. This could occur in as few as several days. If the price continues to move against the trader's position, he could owe his broker even more than the original deposit, which fact makes for high risk taking on the part of the trader. The risk can be substantially reduced (but not eliminated) by using loss-limiting methods such as stop losses, diversification into many other commodities, keeping big money reserves, and using good buy-sell timing methods. These techniques also cut down on profit potential, however.

The remaining two areas are the biggest in both return and risk potential. Horse and other sports betting results in either a good gain or total loss of funds. Usually quickly (for horses) or soon (sports events like football), the bettor will know if he's won or lost money. With pure chance games (poker, craps, state lotteries), the bettor knows within seconds whether he's won or lost everything.

RISK AND REWARD TOGETHER

Risk and return are closely related. Gambling gains can be between two and hundreds of times the initial stake, but the losses are total, and much more frequent. Sports events also pay large returns on average, less than gambling, and losses are normally total. The success rate is usually higher in sporting events than gambling, and compensates for lower returns.

Commodity futures enjoy less risk but produce less gains than in gambling or sports events.

Stocks have potential for many fold increases, but it takes longer than for commodities and occurs less often.

Real estate values can also increase greatly: two- and three-fold increases over a few years is not unheard of. Once in a while, a spectacular boom occurs, such as Las Vegas real estate increasing from $100 per acre before World War II to several hundred thousand dollars recently. These instances (including the old Florida and Arizona land booms) are rare, and sometimes touched with scandal. Usually real estate rates will keep up with those of inflation and population combined.

Corporate bonds and notes pay generally better than bank savings, but are limited in payouts to less than 20% per year. Convertible corporate bonds add a little tickler, and are a bit like a stock or stock option, with a blend of low, fixed return plus growth potential that is tied in with the underlying stock's appreciation.

Bank savings and governmental instruments pay almost the lowest return of all the investment media, albeit they are also very low in risk.

Inflation makes this last category virtually worthless as an investment, because inflation is greater than the returns; hence, purchasing power is reduced and original capital essentially slowly eroded away.

LOW RISK, LOW RETURN; HIGH RETURN, HIGH RISK

If the investor wants higher return potential, he *must* accept higher risk. Conversely, if he wishes to reduce risk, he can only get low returns on his capital. There are no "short cuts": a government bond, with little risk on principal, will not yield 50% a year, with inflation even around 20%. Likewise, roulette winnings can give twenty to one returns for the bet placed, but winning will not occur very often (high risk of loss each time the game is played).

THE POT IS NOT AT THE END OF THE RAINBOW

Contrary to popular belief, the pot of gold (winning investment) is *not* at *either* end of the investment rainbow (Figure 3).

The extremes in investment meet, and are losing propositions in the presence of inflation.

It has been said that the extreme political right and left become identical in results and often in appearance. It can be argued, for instance, that Nazi Germany and the Soviet Union, though different extremes of social and economic philosophy, resemble each other in that the effects on the citizenry are the same: dictatorial conditions, a small ruling group, economic servitude for the masses (either little participation in society's goods, or lack of them for all but a priviledged few), and no freedoms.

In a similar fashion, governmental instruments and others of the lower risk return end of the investment rainbow represent a servitude and slow death to investors' capital. Low rates of return, no matter how safe, are eaten away, and *principal* is eaten into by inflation.

Even when inflation was only 5%, government bonds paid only 3%, or an effective loss of 2% or more each year — a slow but sure death knell on the investor's capital. In high inflation, the "bleeding" or "death" rate is stepped up: instead of 2% loss per year, it might be 10–15%.

In the other extreme, only a very few lucky ones can say they have walked away from a gaming table after playing a lot, and won decisively. The games are rigged. The average person walks away a loser because of the 3% or whatever cut the house takes off the top. After so many plays at the table, the average player is "statistically" cleaned of his stakes: only a few hit long, lucky streaks to go home big winners.

This leaves only the middle ground — from real estate to commodity futures — for the investor to make real progress in profits, or meaningful capital growth.

The task becomes more difficult when inflation heats up. The upper and lower extremes become unbearable (who wants to lose 5–10% per year in bonds, or throw away money in gambling, when it means throwing away even *more* because of inflation).

Even the middle areas become highly unstable and often unprofitable in times of high inflation. Real estate suffers in recession, both pricewise and in the increased illiquidity of assets. Arts and treasures, stamps, and coins suddenly lose their collector appeal because of basic needs to be met first. Hence, demand for and prices of these investments go down drastically. Stocks lose pace to inflation badly (see Figure 1 for no move by stocks and great loss relative to inflation, as measured by the wholesale price index) and behave erratically in recessions and high inflation times. While the wholesale price index climbed steadily from 1959 to 1973, and then accelerated steeply upward from then on, stock prices, as measured by the Dow Jones Industrials, bounced almost regularly from 500 to 1000 and thereupon lost considerably to general prices. Stockholders' assets have lost considerably compared with inflation.

Commodity futures, on the other hand, as a group have not only kept pace with inflation, advancing at an annual rate of almost 20% (see Figure 4, Chapter 3, for the dramatic rise since 1972), but particular commodities have even done better (see Figure 5, Chapter 3, for gold's meteoric rise in 1979 and 1980).

Inflation, then, is the *principal* enemy of the investor. The average investor must not only save money after expenses for rainy days, but *protect* and *multiply* his capital. He must protect it against the ravage of inflation, and make sure it grows at a rate *well above* inflation if he is to make his assets grow in terms of real buying power.

The two extremes are not the answer: the lower end of the investment rainbow *always* loses to inflation, and the upper end is only for enjoyment, again constituting a sure loss of capital (at a quicker pace) except for a very lucky few.

The real answer lies in the middle, and commodity futures is the best media in the middle. The following chapter explains why, and familiarizes the investor with the tools of the trade. Chapter 4 sets forth a practical, simple, but powerful method for capturing profits in commodities. The rest of the chapters concentrate on and explain each commodity and how the method can be used to make profits in each one.

3.
Commodities, From A to Z

In the investment rainbow, commodities are in the higher part of the middle ground — the area offers the highest return with an acceptable risk. Figure 3 recaps its position amongst the many investment choices facing the intrepid investor wishing to beat inflation. Bonds and other "safe" investments lose badly to inflation, because returns on them compare unfavorably with inflation, and are thus slow but sure bloodsuckers on the investor's capital. Wagering represents an easy way to blow all the capital, with only slight hope of tremendous rewards.

Commodities futures, when harnessed, can give most satisfactory returns with relatively controllable risks. As a group it can readily beat inflation. Figure 4 depicts an index of commodity prices for the past twenty-five-odd years. Nothing much happened during low inflation times in the 1950s and 1960s, but inflation increased in the 1970s and so did the value of the commodity index — dramatically rising from 100 in 1971 to over 300 in 1980 — a 200% rise in ten years. This is about *twice* the move of inflation in general (see the wholesale price index for all goods in Figure 1), which went from about 115 to 230 in the same period, only a 100% rise. Not only could you have kept up with inflation, you would have done twice as well, and really prospered.

More importantly, there are individual commodities that even greatly outperformed the huge commodity index rise. Gold, for example, increased from about $40 per ounce to over $800, a 2,000% increase in ten years. And even more fantastic, deposit or margin requirements to buy gold averaged to about 10% of the

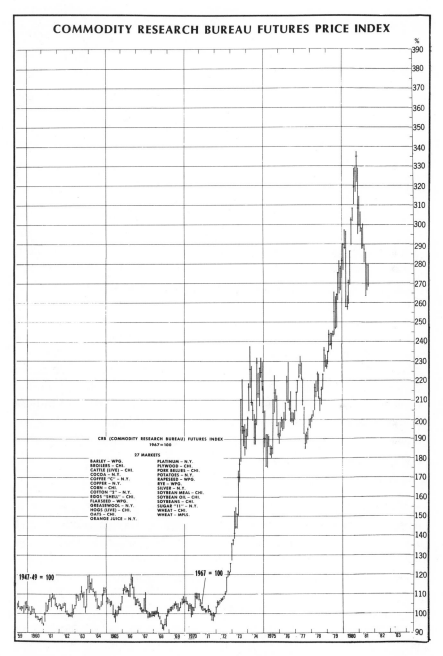

COMMODITY RESEARCH BUREAU FUTURES PRICE INDEX

CRB (COMMODITY RESEARCH BUREAU) FUTURES INDEX
1967 = 100

27 MARKETS

BARLEY – WPG.
BROILERS – CHI.
CATTLE (LIVE) – CHI.
COCOA – N.Y.
COFFEE "C" – N.Y.
COPPER – N.Y.
CORN – CHI.
COTTON "2" – N.Y.
EGGS "SHELL" – CHI.
FLAXSEED – WPG.
GREASEWOOL – N.Y.
HOGS (LIVE) – CHI.
OATS – CHI.
ORANGE JUICE – N.Y.

PLATINUM – N.Y.
PLYWOOD – CHI.
PORK BELLIES – CHI.
POTATOES – N.Y.
RAPESEED – WPG.
RYE – WPG.
SILVER – N.Y.
SOYBEAN MEAL – CHI.
SOYBEAN OIL – CHI.
SOYBEANS – CHI.
SUGAR "11" – N.Y.
WHEAT – CHI.
WHEAT – MPLS.

1947-49 = 100

1967 = 100

Figure 4. (Courtesy of Commodity Research Bureau, Inc., New York, N.Y.)

Figure 5. (Courtesy of Commodity Research Bureau, Inc., New York, N.Y.)

value of the metal, making for a 10 to 1 profit leverage for actual capital put up — or actually 20,000%. (See Figure 5 for gold's price course through the 1970s.) In the extreme, this means a $10,000 investment in gold futures could be worth over $2 million less than ten years later!

COMMODITY FUTURES, A SUPER INVESTMENT MEDIUM

Some examples of supertrends, both up *and* down, are found in Figure 6 (sugar, an enormous uptrend *and* subsequent downtrend). Sugar deposit requirements varied from as low as $1,000 up to $15,000 at the peak in early 1980. A $1,000 deposit on sugar futures would have been worth about $50,000 in early 1980, just *one* year later! Likewise, T-bonds (Figure 7) fell nearly 40 points, or $40,000 per contract, from 1978 to 1980. Margins varied from $1,000 to $4,000 in that time, so an individual could have made almost 40 times his original stake betting on higher interest rates (lower futures prices).

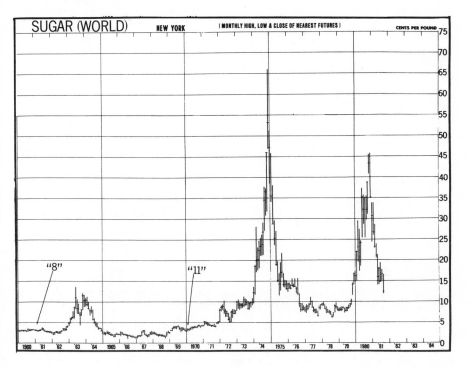

Figure 6. (Courtesy of Commodity Research Bureau, Inc., New York, N.Y.)

Even lowly corn (see Figure 8) can move fast relative to margin requirements in a short time period. From early July to early September, a two-month span, it rose over 60 cents, representing a fivefold profit return on a long position on a 12-cent margin required for a trader lucky enough to have gotten aboard.

Profits can be made no matter what the economic condition of the nation or world — gains on the long side in an inflationary environment with certain commodities, and on the short side in a recession period with particular supply-heavy markets.

However, it takes knowledge of the mechanics of investing or trading in the commodity markets and a good plan to substantially profit in this investment arena.

The balance of the chapter will be devoted to a brief introduction and summary of commodity trading mechanics. More complete

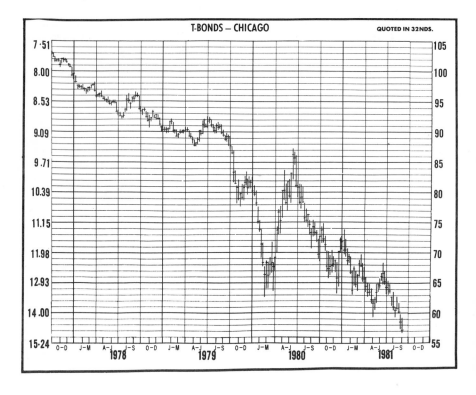

Figure 7. (Courtesy of Commodity Research Bureau, Inc., New York, N.Y.)

discussions can be found in Gold, and Tewles, Harlow and Stone (see reference section at the end of the book).

COMMODITY FUTURES OPERATIONS

The history and need for organized commodity exchanges, and all aspects of the mechanics of trading, are briefly discussed below to aid the investor in understanding this fascinating medium. The procedures and mechanisms from one end of trading to the other — opening an account to tax considerations of final trading results — will be reviewed. Tewles, Harlow, and Stone will be heavily drawn upon for the history and need for commodity exchanges.

Figure 8. (Courtesy of Commodity Research Bureau, Inc., New York, N.Y.)

HISTORY

Trading of commodities on a more formal, organized basis goes back well into time — Chinese, Egyptian, and near-Eastern markets were bustling with bartered and cash-and-carry trading thousands of years ago. The Roman influence made markets more central and credit possible, but it wasn't until the twelfth century in France that bargains were struck for future delivery of goods. A *lettre de faire,* or something equivalent to a modern warehouse receipt, let buyers close out a deal on specific goods at a specific agreed upon price for delivery of the goods at a later date. The Royal Exchange in London, opened in 1570, brought many merchants together on a year-round basis and concentrated trading in a central place. The merchants bought and sold the actual goods with cash, but increasingly used forward contracts, the forerunner of our futures contracts, to lock in amounts and prices of goods for some future time. A merchant may have wished to have a supply of wool available to him in the spring so that a consumer of his, a manufacturer of woolen goods, could purchase an adequate supply from the merchant.

While trading in forward contracts has been carried on in England for many centuries now, futures contracts have only been in existence here in the United States for a little over a hundred years. The Chicago Board of Trade, established in 1848, was the first. Grain-related commodities were traded first, with other commodities added there and at other exchanges later on.

Then, and even today, most agricultural goods produced in the United States were transported centrally through Chicago, while New York captured futures trading in most of the internationally produced goods, such as sugar and cocoa. Ten or more major exchanges now trade over fifty commodities, ranging from cattle to wheat and cocoa to Treasury bonds. The volume of trading contracts increased nearly *fivefold* from 1954 to 1972, and the dollar volume has increased almost *tenfold* from $200 billion in 1972 to over $2 trillion in 1981.

WHY THE NEED FOR COMMODITY FUTURES EXCHANGES?

Serious debates have gone on in Congress and acrimony has arisen on the part of some producers, users, and the investing public that the exchanges serve no real useful purpose for the country and only constitute another gambling outlet for those so inclined. Tewles (pp. 13–15 and 46) cites arguments and studies that show that, at the least, the existence of exchanges does not harm the underlying cash markets for the commodities and probably even dampens the price swings and volatility in these marketplaces.

Basically, the need for exchanges comes from the need of hedgers, both producers and users of basic goods, to offset risks in their normal business. The quality and quantity of wheat grown in a crop year will depend much on weather. Demand for wheat will depend upon national and international demand, which will also be influenced by governmental and other human influences, such as the U.S. freeze in early 1980 on grain exports to Russia.

None of these variables are controllable by the farmer or miller or baking companies. One or more factors may pull down the price for the farmer, far below what he wanted at harvest time. Under that circumstance, he would lose much of the income he had counted on, to even meet bills and keep the farm going. He can turn to the commodity futures markets to sell his wheat before prices begin to fall, even though he doesn't have it harvested yet. He is contracting to the futures market for delivering the wheat at a later date, not at the present time. Later, at harvest time, he can deliver the wheat he has contracted to sell in the futures markets, or buy back the contract he made and sell his harvested wheat in the real marketplace.

Normally, the only time the farmer can reap the benefits of his work is at harvest time, when he gets cold cash for the entire year's work. Rather than chancing everything on one date, he can turn to the futures markets and have the opportunity to pick different times during the year to realize, or lock in, part or all of his crop at prices that allow him to prosper. This way the futures markets can be used as an *insurance* vehicle, to insure he won't receive any lower than a set price for his crop. For that he pays two prices, commissions to transact the futures contracts (usually very low in relation to the value traded), and the possible opportunity to get a better price later on at harvest time (when perhaps a drought has occurred and prices are very high).

In a similar vein, users of raw commodities would not like to see prices skyrocket, otherwise they probably would have to pass on extra costs to the consumer. Users could make more profits by keeping effective prices they pay for these raw goods down. A cocoa manufacturer, for example, could buy cocoa futures and make money in that market as prices rose, to offset additional costs of actually procuring the brown beans at later dates. Not only could he offset the extra cash cost with futures gain, but he could even gain more revenue by offering the candy bar at lower prices than competitors who did *not* use the futures markets, and getting more sales that way.

The futures markets must be liquid and smoothly price-behaved for producers and users to obtain fair, usable prices, and hence the need for speculators. When farmers go to the futures market, they want to be sure their sales will not drive the prices down abnormally (compared to normal fluctuations in the cash markets, that is), and likewise for baking companies who use the farmers goods, who don't want to see their (the bakers') buying unsettle the market much on the upside.   Most of the time, however, there are not offsetting, equally influencing buying and selling hedgers – the farmers and hedgers don't come together at the same instant – and so there is a need for some offsetting buying or absorbing influence to sell when users come in to buy.   Speculators absorb both buying and selling at different times to make the market more orderly, prices smoother, at times of excess selling and buying.

While this discussion sounds plausible, the proof is in the pudding. The central argument revolves around the problem of deciding what is a "fair" price for any good at any time.   In our capitalistic society, we have agreed that "the market forces" must determine that, without undue coercive outside influences, whether private or public manipulation or setting of fixed prices.   This is the cornerstone of free enterprise, that the real unfettered forces of supply and demand determine prices in an auction market.

"Market forces" in commodities have come to mean the effects on cash prices.   There, supply and demand meet head on and a compromise price is agreed upon.   But for those users and producers of the commodities who can only go into the cash market once a year or infrequently, the economic consequences can be bad.   The farmer could only sell at the very low price of the year (harvest time) in a bumper crop year or, in the case of the baker, at the very high price if the crop had experienced a drought.   The futures markets allow *continuous* buying and selling all year long on the part of *all* hedgers, producers and users, to, in effect, allow them to average out or preselect satisfactory prices for their products.

The above discussion and examples were simplified.   The marketplaces' participants and influences are far more complicated: a hedger must consider many, many factors – cost of inventory, expected events, planning his organization's growth, capital needs, to name just a few.

Make no mistake about it, the commodities markets would not exist and be viable without real hedger need and the liquidity made available by speculators.   Most markets, like the grains, have strong counterbalancing forces – about equal strength in hedging and speculation. Also, futures prices reflect cash prices, the primary market buying and selling is based upon, in a very close manner.

Once in a while, a market will become unbalanced and even unworkable. Speculation on pork bellies in the late sixties and seventies was such a high proportion of trading that the markets "dried up" — very little volume and erratic prices resulted. Similarly, in 1980 silver trading was so influenced by speculative appeal that prices went crazy. Margins had to be increased to dampen prices (keep them orderly), so that volume shrunk to a mere pittance of former levels. Many markets have become extinct. However, because of lack of hedger interest; tom turkey, tomato paste, apples, rice and so on have bit the dust after brief existences. Hedgers have had their day in court, not as spectacularly but nearly as influencing. Cocoa and coffee are greatly influenced by a few producer nations who have been known to conspire as trusts to keep prices up, and to obscure and even falsify crop condition reports to the disadvantage of users in the U.S. Potato producers several years ago had a gigantic poker and gunslinger party at the end of the trading year, to see who had what first (who had gone short and long and how much), and then to see how much they could run up or down the prices. There followed a "shoot-out" on the last day of trading — to see who had the stamina and resources to outlast the others.

Probably the most celebrated "cornering of the market," besides the silver debacle, was the buying up of grain by exporters for shipment to Russia at much higher prices, to the dismay and economic loss of farmers had they known the situation. In secrecy, the exporters bought low on the exchanges, turned around and sold high — much like the oil cartel arrangements now, only in reverse — and with a captive American economy to boot, with oil companies profiting from a conspiring seller. Fortunately, for the general speculative public, the U.S. government from 1973 on has made the grain market news more open.

THE MECHANICS OF TRADING

An individual or organization contemplating trading commodities can do so by opening an account with two types of firms: firms specializing in commodities only, the majority of which are located in Chicago with branch offices in major U.S. cities; and general financial brokerage houses, which deal in many financial instruments and are generally located throughout the U.S. Physically, the branch and main offices are like many retail paper-oriented businesses — small, having many desks, cubicles or offices, and a lot of communication equipment.   Telephones are used for calling clients and placing orders.   Quotation machines tell the broker and his customer the history and current status of prices for any commodity in question, and other equipment is used to transmit orders, and to print out financial records of trading and other account information.   Advisory information is available, through published weekly and other letters, and verbally from squawk boxes and the broker.   Not only should a potential client judge the physical attributes of the prospective firm, but he should scrutinize the organizational abilities: Are orders executed well?   Is it financially sound?   To name a few.

OPENING THE ACCOUNT

To open an account, several documents must be signed.   A general agreement stipulates that the client will be responsible for margin calls and debits in his account and will generally abide by the rules of the various exchanges.   Some will ask the customer to allow the brokerage to transfer funds from one type of account (cash, money funds, securities accounts, for example) to another, for meeting margins and debit situations.   An option is to have the client agree to arbitrate any differences that might arise before a nationwide arbitration group of the bar association for fair settlement.   An accompanying document, a risk disclosure statement, is required to be signed by the CFTC (Commodity Futures Trading Commission, the federal government regulatory body similar in function to the Securities and Exchange Commission) to show that the client understands the leveraged, risk-taking nature of commodities.

Personal information, including financial status, of the client is asked for on other forms.   If the customer has someone else exercising discretion or authority (decision-making or the ability to transfer or remove funds), a trading or other authorization form is needed. Finally, if the client is a corporation, a copy of the corporate chapter and a resolution allowing the company to trade will be required.

A deposit of funds is the next step. Many firms have minimum account size requirements, ranging from just a few thousand dollars for small, Chicago-based houses to $50,000 or more for managed accounts for larger firms.

Next, of course, the customer must determine *what* he will trade in, *when* he will trade, *how* he can transact the trade, and *where* the transaction will take place.

The first two questions, the what and when, form the basis for the bulk of this book: what to buy or sell, and the timing of the trade. The following will be a cursory discussion of the basic mechanics of transacting a trade, while the rest of the book will be devoted to developing and implementing a good program for trading commodities.

COMMODITY FUTURES FACTS

Table 1 is a listing of commodity futures traded and associated facts: where the commodity is traded, trading hours, contract size, minimum price changes, and so on.

Commodities are traded in units of thousands of pounds, bushels, or ounces, similar to a unit of 100 shares of stock exchanges. Each exchange has a price change minimum between upward or downward price moves for each commodity, which translates into certain dollar changes when calculated on the contract size. Cattle price *changes* must be at least .025 cents per pound either up or down from the last price, or .025 cents times 40,000 lbs. in the contract, which equals $10. For comparison purposes, the value of a one-cent move on 40,000 lbs. of cattle would be $.01 × 40,000, or $400. The exchanges also prohibit trading at prices above a maximum price and below a minimum price, which prices are arrived at by taking the prior close price and adding the maximum price change allowed to obtain the maximum, and subtracting to obtain the minimum. For example, if cattle closed at 60.00 cents a pound today, trading would be limited to 60.00 + 1.50 = 61.50 cents maximum, 60.00 – 1.50 = 58.50 minimum tomorrow. The purpose of this arbitrary device – stopping trading at certain limits – is to prevent the possibility of manipulative or panic price moves that could lead to huge price changes that could bankrupt the client whose position wad adversely affected by the price change. If cattle prices were allowed to fall unchecked to 30.00 from 60.00 cents in the day, for

Table 1.

United States

	Trading Hours (Local Time)	Contract Unit	Minimum Price Change Per Unit	Per Contract
Imported Lean Beef NYMEX	10:15- 1:45	36,000 Lbs	2¢ cwt	$ 7.20
Broilers, Frozen Fresh CME	9:10- 1:00	30,000 Lbs	2 1/2¢ 100¢ Lb	$ 7.50
Cattle, Midwestern CME	9:05-12.45	40,000 Lbs	2 1/2¢ 100¢ Lb	$ 10.00
Cattle, Midwestern MACE	9:05- 1:00	20,000 Lbs	.00025¢ Lb	$ 5.00
Citrus (FCOJ) NYCE	10:15- 2:45	15,000 Lbs	5/100¢ Lb	$ 7.50
Cocoa NYCSC	9:30- 2:55	10 Metric Tons	$1 Metric Ton	$ 10.00
Coffee C NYCSC	9:45- 2:28	37,500 Lbs	$ 1/100¢ Lb	$ 3.75
Copper COMEX	9:50- 2:00	25,000 Lbs	05/100¢ Lb	$ 12.50
Corn CBT	9:30- 1:15	5000 Bus	1/4¢ Bu	$ 12.50
Corn MACE	9:30- 1:15	1000 Bus	1/8¢ Bu	$ 1.25
Cotton NYCE	10:30- 3:00	50,000 Lbs	$ 1/100¢ Lb	$ 5.00
Currencies, Foreign IMM				
British Pound	7:30- 1:24	25,000	.0005	$ 12.50
Canadian Dollar	1:22	100,000	.0001	$ 10.00
Deutschemark	1:20	125,000	.0001	$ 12.50
Dutch Guilder	1:30	125,000	.0001	$ 12.50
French Franc	1:28	250,000	.0005	$ 12.50
Japanese Yen	1:26	12,500,000	.00001	$ 12.50
Mexican Peso	1:18	1,000,000	.00001	$ 12.50
Swiss Franc	1:16	125,000	.0001	$ 12.50
Feeder Cattle CME	9:05-12:45	42,000 Lbs	$ .000025 Lb	$ 10.50
Gold CBT	8:25- 1:35	100 Tr Oz	10¢ Oz	$ 10.00
Gold COMEX	9:25- 1:35	100 Tr Oz	10¢ Oz	$ 10.00
Gold IMM	8:25- 1:30	100 Tr Oz	10¢ Oz	$ 10.00
Gold MACE	8:25- 1:40	33.2 Tr Oz	2.5¢ Oz	$ .83
GNMA CDR CBT	8:00- 2:00	$100,000	1/32 Pt	$ 31.25
GNMA CD CBT	8:00- 2:00	$100,000	1/32 Pt	$ 31.25
Hogs, Live CME	9:10- 1:00	30,000 Lbs	2 1/2 100¢ Lb	$ 7.50
Hog, Live MACE	9:10- 1:15	15,000 Lbs	.025¢ Lb	$ 3.75
Lumber CME	9:00- 1:05	130,000 BD Ft	10¢ MBF	$ 13.00
Lumber, Stud CME	9:00- 1:05	100,000 BD Ft	10¢ MBF	$ 10.00
Oats CBT	9:30- 1:15	5,000 Bus	1/4¢ Bu	$ 12.50
Oats MACE	9:30- 1:30	5,000 Bus	1/8¢ Bu	$ 6.25
#2 Heating Oil NYMEX	10:30- 2:45	42,000 US GALS	$ .0001 GAL	$ 4.20
Palladium NYMEX	9:50- 2:20	100 Tr Oz	5¢ Tr Oz	$ 5.00
Platinum NYMEX	9:30- 2:30	50 Tr Oz	10¢ Tr Oz	$ 5.00
Plywood CBT	9:00- 1:00	76,032 Sqft	10¢ MSF	$ 7.60
Plywood, Western CBT	9:00- 1:00	76,032 Sqft	10¢ MSF	$ 7.60
Pork Bellies	9:10- 1:00	38,000 Lbs	$ .00025 Lb	$ 9.50
Potatoes, Red White	10:00- 2:00	50,000 Lbs	1¢ cwt.	$ 5.00
Potatoes, Russet Burbank CME	9:00- 12:50	80,000 Lbs	1¢ cwt.	$ 8.00

Table 1. (Continued)

Value Of 1¢/1$ Move	Maximun Daily Price Change	Price Range	Contract Value Of Maximum Move	Trading Limit Notes
$ 360.	$1.50	$3.00	$ 540.	$2 & $4 During Delivery Month
$ 300.	2¢	4¢	$ 600.	No Limit On Spot Month During Delivery Month
$ 400.	1 1/2¢	3¢	$ 600.	
$ 200.	1 1/2¢	3¢	$ 300.	
$ 150.	5¢	10¢	$ 750.	No Limit On Spot Month On And After 8th Day
$ 10.	$ 88	$ 176.	$ 880.	No Limit On Spot Month On And After 8th Day
$ 375.	4¢	8¢	$1500.	No Limit On Spot Month In Notice Period
$ 250.	5¢	10¢	$1250.	No Limit O Spot On & After Day Prior to FND
$ 50.	10¢	20¢	$ 500.	
$ 10.	10¢	20¢	$ 100.	
$ 500.	2¢	4¢	$1000.	No Limit On Spot Month On & After FND
	.05	.1000	$1200.	
	.0075	.0150	$ 750.	
	.01	.0200	$1250.	
	.01	.0200	$1250.	No Limit On Spot Month Beginning
	.005	.010	$1250.	On Day Previous Month Expires
	.0001	.0002	$1250.	
	.0015	.003	$1500.	
	.015	.03	$1875.	
$ 420.	1 1/2¢	3¢	$ 630.	
$ 100.	$40.00	$ 80.00	$4000.	
$ 100.	$25.00	$ 50.00	$2500.	No Limit On Spot Month During Delivery Month
$ 100.	$50.00	$ 100.00	$5000.	No Limit In Spot Month During Delivery Period
$33.20	$25.00	$ 50.00	$ 830.	No Limit On Spot Month During Delivery Month
1 Pt=$1000	64/32nds	128/32nds	$2000.	No Limit On Spot Month During Delivery Period
1 Pt=$1000	64/32nds	128/32nds	$2000.	No Limit On Spot Month During Delivery Period
$ 300.	1 1/2¢	3¢	$ 450.	
$ 150.	1 1/2¢	3¢	$ 225.	
$ 130.	$ 5.00	$ 10.00	$ 850.	
$ 100.	$ 5.00	$ 10.00	$ 500.	
$ 50.	6¢	12¢	$ 300.	
$ 50.	6¢	12¢	$ 300.	
$ 420.	2¢	4¢	$ 840.	Limit Off In Month Prior To Delivery Month
$ 100.	$ 6.00	$ 12.00	$ 600.	No Limit On Last Trading Day
$ 50.	$20.00	$ 40.00	$1000.	No Limit On Last Trading Day
$ 76.	$ 7.00	$ 14.00	$ 532.	No Limit On Spot Month On And After FND
$ 76.	$ 7.00	$ 14.00	$ 532.	
$ 380.	$ .02	$ .04	$ 760.	
$ 5.	.50¢	$ 1.00	$ 250.	No Limit On LTD
$ 8.	.50¢	$ 1.00	$ 400.	$1 & $2 On LTD

Table 1. (Continued)

United States

	Trading Hours (Local Time)	Contract Unit	Minimum Price Change Per Unit	Per Contract
Rice, Milled NOCE	9:45- 1:45	1200 cwt.	$ .005 cwt.	$ 6.00
Rice, Rough NOCE	9:45- 1:45	2000 cwt.	$ .005 cwt.	$10.00
Silver COMEX	9:40- 2:15	5000 Tr Oz	10/100¢ Oz	$ 5.00
Silver CBT	8:40- 1:25	5000 Tr Oz	10/100¢ Oz	$ 5.00
Silver CBT	8:40- 1:25	1000 Tr Oz	10/100¢ Oz	$ 1.00
Silver MACE	8:40- 1:40	1000 Tr Oz	.05¢ Oz	$ 2.00
Silver Coins IMM	8:50- 1:25	$5000 Face Value 5 Bags	$ 1 Bag	$ 5.00
Soybeans CBT	9:30- 1:15	5000 Bus	1/4¢ Bu	$12.50
Soybeans MACE	9:30- 1:30	1000 Bus	1/8¢ Bu	$ 1.25
Soybean Meal CBT	9:30- 1:15	100 Tons (200,000 Lbs)	10¢ Ton	$10.00
Soybean Oil CBT	9:30- 1:15	60,000 Lbs	1/100¢ Lb	$ 6.00
Sunflowerseed MPLS	9:25- 1:20	100,000 Lbs	$ .001 Lb	$ .10
Sugar #11 NYCSC	10:00- 1:43	112,000 Lbs	1/00¢ Lb	$11.20
Sugar #12 NYCSC	10:00- 1:43	112,000 Lbs	1/00¢ Lb	$11.20
Treasury Bills' (90 Day) IMM	8:00- 1:40	$1,000,000 Face Value	1 Basis Pt .01	$25.00
Treasury Bills (90 Day) NYFE	9:00- 3:00	$1,000,000 Face Value	1 Basis Pt .01	$25.00
Treasury Bonds CBT	8:00- 2:00	$ 1000,000 at 8%	1/32 Pt	$31.25
Treasury Bonds NYFE	9:00- 3:00	$ 1000,000 at 8%	1/32 Pt	$31.25
Treasury Notes (2 Yr) COMEX	9:00- 3:00	$ 1000,000 at 8%	1/64 Pt	$15.25
Treasury Notes (4-6 Yrs) CBT	8:00- 2:00	$ 1000,000	1/32 Pt	$31.25
Wheat CBT - KC - MPLS	9:00- 1:15	5000 Bus	1/4¢ Bu	$12.50
Wheat MACE	9:30- 1:30	1000 Bus	1/8¢ Bu	$ 1.25

¹ Daily price changes on both CBT and MACE Silver are based on price.

When price less than $ 9.00 —
$ 9.00 but less than $15.00 —
$15.00 but less than $20.00 —
$20.00 and above   —

Table 1. (Continued)

Value Of 1¢/1$ Move	Maximum Daily Price Change	Price Range	Contract Value Of Maximum Move	Trading Limit Notes
	.50¢	$ 1.00	$ 600.	
	.30¢	$ 60¢	$ 600.	
50.00	.50¢	$ 1.00	$2500.	No Ltd On & After Day Prior to FND
50.00	.40¢[1]	80¢[1]	$2000.	No Ltd During Notice Period
10.00	.40¢[1]	80¢[1]	$ 400.	No Ltd During Notice Period
10.00	.40¢[1]	80¢[1]	$ 400.	No Ltd During Notice Period
5.00	$ 150.	$ 300	$ 750.	
50.00	30¢	60¢	$1500.	
10.00	30¢	60¢	$ 300.	
)0.	$ 10.00	$ 20.00	$1000.	No Ltd On Spot Month On & After FND
)0	1¢	2¢	$ 600.	No Ltd On Spot Month On & After FND
)0.	$ .005	$ .01	$ 500.	
?0.	1¢	2¢	$1120.	No Ltd On Spot Month
?0.	1¢	2¢	$1120.	No Ltd On Spot Month
) Basis Pts=$2500	Basis Pts .50	100 Basis Pts	$1250.	No Ltd On Spot Month
) Basis Pts=$2500	Basis Pts .50		$2500.	
#2nds= $1000	64/32nds	128/32nds	$2000.	
32nds= $1000	96/32nds		$3000.	No Ltd On Spot Month During Del Mo.
54ths= $1000	64/64ths	128/64ths	$1000.	
32nds= $1000	64/32nds	128/32nds	$2000.	
	20¢ CHIC & MPLS	40¢	$1000 CHIC & MPLS	
	25¢ KC	50¢	$1500 KC	
,00	20¢	40¢	$ 200.	
,00				
per oz. - 40¢ range				
per oz. - 80¢ range				
per oz. - 120¢ range				
per oz. - 160¢ range				

Table 1. (Continued)

COMMODITY AND EXCHANGE	TRADING HOURS LOCAL TIME	CONTRACT UNIT
Lead-London LME (See LME footnote)	12:10-12:13, 12:45-12:50, 15:30-15:35, 16:00-16:05, 13:15-13:25, 16:40-17:00 (KERB)	25 Metric Tons
Nickel-London LME (See LME footnote)	12:20-12:25, 13:00-13:05, 15:45-15:50, 16:30-16:35, 13:15-13:25, 16:40-17:00 (KERB)	6 Metric Tons
Rubber-London Rubber Term Mkt Assoc	8:45-09:30 Kerb 9:45-12:45 14:30-17:05	15 Tons (5 Tons Per Mo in 3 Mon Period)
Silver-London LME (See LME footnote)	11:50-11:55, 13:05-13:10, 15:50-15:55, 16:35-16:40, 13:15-13:25, 16:40-17:00 (KERB)	10,000 Troy Ounces
Soybean Meal-London Gafta Soyameal Fut Mkt	10:30-12:20, 14:30-17:00 Kerb After Official Call Until 19:15	100 Metric Tons (1000 Kilos Each
Sugar-London White Unit Term Sug Mkt Assoc	10:30-12:30, 14:30-17:00 17:00-20:00, (KERB)	50 Metric Tons
Sugar-London Mkt Assoc Unit Term Sug Mkt Assoc	10:30-12:30, 14:30-17:00 17:00-20:00 (KERB)	50 Metric Tons
Sugar-London Raws #4 Unit Term Sug Mkt Assoc	10:30-12:30, 14:30-17:00 17:00-20:00 (KERB)	50 Metric Tons
Tin-London LME (See LME footnote)	Kerb 13:15, 13:25 12:05-12:10, 12:40-12:45 Kerb 16:40, 17:00 15:40-15:45, 16:20-16:25	5 Metric Tons
Zinc-London LME (See LME footnote)	12:15-12:20, 12:50-12:55, 15:30-15:35, 16:05-16:10, 13:15-13:25, 16:40-17:00 (KERB)	25 Metric Tons
Gas Oil In Bulk Intl Pet Ex of London	09:30-12:30 02:45-05:20	100 Tons

LME Metals footnote

There is both pre and after market hours trading in all the LME metals
(copper, tin, lead, zinc, aluminim, nickel, and silver). It is
therefore possible to trade in all these metals from 08:30 AM - 19:30 PM.
 Trading is definitely not confined to the official trading
 times stated on the sheet.

Table 1. (Continued)

	MINIMUM PRICE CHANGE		VALUE OF 1¢/$1/L1	MAXIMUM DAILY		TRADING LIMIT
PER UNIT		PER CONTRACT	MOVE	PRICE CHANGE	PRICE RANGE	NOTES
	L.25	L6.25	L.25	None	None	
L.1 Tons		L .6	L.6	None	None	
0.10 Pence Kilo		L1.50	–	3 Pence	None	
.05P Troy Ounces				None		
L.100 Tons		L.10	L.100		L5.00	
L. 5 Tons		L.25		L.20	L.40	No Limit On Spot Month
L.5 Tons		L.25		L.20	L.40	No Limit On Spot Month
L.5 Tons		L.25		L.20	L.40	No Limit On Spot Month
L.1 Tons		L.5		None	None	
L.25 Tons		L.6		None	None	
25¢ US Tons		$25		$30	None	

Table 1. (Continued)

London / Sydney

COMMODITY AND EXCHANGE	TRADING HOURS LOCAL TIME	CONTRACT UNIT
Aluminum, London	Kerb 13:15-13:25 11:55-12:00, 12:55-13:00 Kerb 16:40-17:00	25 Metric
LME (See LME footnote)	15:45-15:50, 16:25-16:30	Tons
Cocoa-London Cocoa	10:00-13:00	10 Metric
Terminal Mkt Assoc	14:30-16:45	(1,000 KGS)
Coffee London Robusta	10:30-12:30	5 Metric
Coffee Term Mkt Assoc	14:30-17:00	Tons
Coffee No. 2 Arabica	10:15-16:45	17,250 Kilos
Coffee Term Mkt Assoc		(250 Bags of 69 Kilos)
Copper-High Grade LME (See LME footnote) Standard	12:00-12:05, 12:30-12:35, 15:35-15:40, 16:10-16:15, 13:15-13:25, 16:40-17:00 (KERB) 12:00-12:05, 16:15-16:20,	25 Metric Tons
Copper-Catnodes LME (See LME footnote)	15:35-15:40, 16:15-16:20, 13:15-13:25, 16:40-17:00 (KERB)	25 Metric Tons
Gold-London Bullion	08:30-19:30 Fixes Held At 10:30 AM 15:00 PM (See Footnote)	Min. Order Outside Of Fixes is 400 Ozs Min. Order for Fixes are 100 Ozs Min. Order for Covering vs Amsterdam Mkt is 10 Ozs (See footnote)

GOLD BULLION FOOTNOTE: WE DO NOT OPERATE A DESK SERVICE BETWEEN 19:30 PM AND 8:30 AM BUT ORDERS CAN BE TAKEN THROUGH THE DAY FOR EXECUTION ON HONG KONG DURING THE HOURS THAT THERE IS NO DESK SERVICE IN LONDON.

Silver-London Bullion	08:30-19:30 Fix held At 12:15	Min. Order is 5000 Ozs Min. Order for Daily Fix 1000 Ozs See Gold Bullion Footnote
Crossbred, Greasy Wool #2 Ldn Wool Term Mkt Assoc	10:30-12:00,15:00-16:30, Kerb Until 17:30	1500 Kilos
Greasy Wool Sydney	11:00-12:30 15:00-16:30	1500 Kilos

Table 1. (Continued)

MINIMUM PRICE CHANGE PER UNIT	PER CONTRACT	VALUE OF 1¢/$1/L1 MOVE	MAXIMUM PRICE CHANGE	DAILY PRICE RANGE	TRADING LIMIT NOTES
L.5	L.25	L.25	None	None	
L.1 Tons	L.10	L.10	L.40	None	
L.1 Tons	L. 5	L. 5	None	None	
$ .05 50 Kilos	$17.25	$3.45	None	None	
L.5 Tons	L12.5	L.25	None	None	
L.5 Tons	L12.5	L.25	None	None	
NA	NA	NA	None	None	
NA	NA	NA	None	None	
1 Pence Kilo					
.10¢ Per Kilo	$ 1.50 Aust				

Table 1. (Continued)

Canada

	Trading Hours (Local Time)	Contract Unit	Minimum Price Change Per Unit	Per Contract
Barley - Domestic Feed WGE	9:30- 1:15	100 Tons (BDLOT)		$ 20.00
		20 Tons (JOBLOT)	10¢ Ton	$100. CDN
Flaxseed WGE	9:30- 1:15	100 Tons (BD LOT)		$ 20.00
		20 Tons (JOB LOT)	10¢ Ton	$100. CDN
Oats - Domestic Feed WGE	9:30- 1:15	100 Tons (BD LOT)		$ 20.00
		20 Tons (JOB LOT)	10¢ Ton	$100. CDN
Rye WGE	9:30- 1:15	100 Tons (BD LOT)		$ 20.00
		20 Tons (JOB LOT)	10¢ Ton	$100. CDN
Rapseed-Vancouver WGE	9:30- 1:15	100 Tons (BD LOT)		$ 20.00
		20 Tons (JOB LOT)	10¢ Ton	$100. CDN
Wheat-Domestic Feed WGE	9:30- 1:15	100 Tons (BD LOT)		$ 20.00
		20 Tons (JOB LOT)	10¢ Ton	$100. CDN
Treasury Bills (90 Day)	9:30- 3:15	$ 1,000,000	1 Basis Pt	
Toronto Stock Exchange		Board Lot	.01	$25.00 CDN
Gold - Toronto	8:25- 1:30	20 Ozs	10¢ Oz	$ 2.00
Silver Toronto	8:40- 1:25	200 Ozs	1¢ Oz	$ 2.00
Treasury Bonds TSE	9:30- 3:15	$1000,000 at 9%	$ 31.25	$31.25

Hong Kong / Kuala Lumpur

COMMODITY AND EXCHANGE	TRADING HOURS LOCAL TIME	CONTRACT UNIT
Cotton	9:45-11:15	
Hong Kong Cmdy Ex	15:00-16:30	50,000 LBs
Soybeans	4 Sessions	
Hong Kong	9:50 AM, 10:50 AM, 12:50 PM, 02:50 PM	500 Bags of 60 Kgs
Sugar	10:15-11:45	50 Long Tons
Hong Kong	14:30-16:00	(112,000 LBs
Gold	9:00-12:00	
Hong Kong	14:30-17:30	100 Tr Oz
Palm Oil-Kuala Lumpur	11:00-12:30	25 Metric
Kuala Lumpur Cmdy Ex	3:30- 6:00	Tons

Table 1. (Continued)

Value Of 1¢/1$ Move	Maximum Daily Price Change	Price Range	Contract Value Of Maximum Move
$ 20.			$ 100
$ 100.	$ 5.00	$ 10.00	$ 500.
$ 20.			$ 200
$ 100.	$ 10.00	$ 20.00	$1000.
$ 20.			$ 200
$ 100.	$ 5.00	$ 10.00	$1000.
$ 20.			$ 100
$ 100.	$ 5.00	$ 10.00	$5000.
$ 20.			$ 200
$ 100.	$ 10.00	$ 20.00	$1000.
$ 20.			$ 100
$ 100.	$ 5.00	$ 10.00	$1000.
100 Basis Pts=$2500	60 Basis Pt .60	120 Basis Pts 120	$1500.
$ 20.00	$ 30.00	$ 60	$ 600.
$ 2.00	$ 50¢	$ 1.00	$ 100.
$32nd $1000	$ 64/34nds	$128/32nds	$ 2000

MINIMUM PRICE CHANGE PER UNIT	PER CONTRACT	VALUE OF 1¢/$1/L1 MOVE	MAXIMUM DAILY PRICE CHANGE	PRICE RANGE	TRADING LIMIT NOTES
1/100¢ US Lb	$ 5.00				
20 HK¢					
1/100¢ US	$11.20				
10¢ US					
10¢ US	$10.00				
$1 Malaysia	$25.00 Malaysia		1st day − $ 5.00 2nd day − $ 75.00 3rd day − $100.00 4th day − None 5th day − $ 50.00		

instance, the buyer of a cattle contract would be out $.30 X 40,000 lbs. = $12,000, with margin (deposit) requirements of only $1,500, for example.

PRICE LISTING

Some representative daily prices – open, high, low, close – change from prior closing prices, and open interest (number of trades still outstanding) are shown in Figure 9, a futures prices listing from *The New York Times*. May wheat on March 15, 1982 rose on the close by 6.25 cents, or $50/cents X 6.25 = $312.50 from the prior day's closing price. The volume of sales for the day in all contract months of wheat was 12,068 units (contracts).

Figure 10 is a sample of a coffee contract that spells out exactly what is being traded, where it is to be delivered if such is the case,

—Season—						Open
High	Low	High	Low	Close	Chg.	Interest

WHEAT (CBT) 5,000 bu.; $ per bu.

5.38	3.37½	Mar	3.43	3.36½	3.42¾	+.05¼	1,201
5.26	3.45¼	May	3.53	3.45	3.52¾	+.06¼	17,410
4.97½	3.58¾	Jul	3.65½	3.57	3.65	+.06	21,344
5.02	3.72½	Sep	3.78¾	3.71½	3.78½	+.05½	5,102
5.01	3.89½	Dec	3.95½	3.89	3.95½	+.04¼	3,675
4.58	4.04¼	Mar	4.09¼	4.03½	4.09¼	+.03	1,164

Est. sales 12,068. Prev. sales 22,131.
Prev day's open Int 49,896, off 1,325.

SILVER (CBT)
5,000 troy oz.; ¢ per troy oz.

870.0	690.0	Mar	.....	.....	724.0	+25.0	.....
4562.0	690.0	Apr	727.0	695.0	727.0	+25.0	546
795.0	713.0	May	736.0	711.0	736.0	+25.0	3
4580.0	710.0	Jun	745.0	710.0	745.0	+25.0	1,089
4836.0	730.0	Aug	763.0	729.0	763.0	+25.0	590
3060.0	750.0	Oct	781.0	750.0	781.0	+25.0	488
3120.0	765.0	Dec	799.0	763.0	799.0	+25.0	651
2728.0	810.0	Feb	.....	.....	817.0	+25.0	804
2674.0	810.0	Apr	835.0	810.0	835.0	+25.0	1,127
2166.0	830.0	Jun	853.0	815.0	853.0	+25.0	701
1681.0	845.0	Aug	.....	.....	871.0	+25.0	248
1684.5	862.0	Oct	.....	.....	889.0	+25.0	166

Est. sales 201. Prev. sales 143.
Prev day's open Int 6,413, up 12.

GOLD (NYCX) 100 troy oz.; $ per troy oz.

418.00	319.00	Mar	315.00	312.00	324.20	+6.40	43
898.00	317.50	Apr	327.00	312.50	326.20	+6.60	40,862
.....	.....	May	328.00	328.00	329.70	+6.70	.....
925.10	324.50	Jun	335.50	319.00	333.30	+6.80	32,391
887.00	332.00	Aug	341.50	327.00	340.60	+7.00	17,726
841.00	339.00	Oct	347.00	333.00	347.90	+7.20	18,209
658.00	346.00	Dec	357.00	340.00	355.40	+7.30	10,814
642.00	355.00	Feb	363.00	347.50	363.30	+7.50	17,348
604.00	361.50	Apr	373.70	355.50	371.40	+7.70	9,659
596.00	379.00	Jun	370.50	365.50	379.70	+7.90	2,009
515.50	380.00	Aug	371.00	371.00	388.00	+8.10	868
500.00	392.00	Oct	388.00	388.00	396.50	+8.30	566
495.00	405.00	Dec	399.00	385.00	405.00	+8.50	61

Est. sales 65,000. Prev. sales 61,222.
Prev day's open Int 150,374, off 341.

—Season—						Open
High	Low	High	Low	Close	Chg.	Interest

U.S. TREASURY BILLS (CME)
$1 million; pts. of 100%

91.92	85.09	Mar	87.37	87.06	87.24	-.09	3,627
91.38	85.40	Jun	87.38	86.98	87.22	-.10	20,715
89.70	85.43	Sep	87.10	86.77	86.96	-.07	6,822
89.49	85.73	Dec	86.96	86.70	86.85	-.04	3,189
88.85	85.77	Mar	86.85	86.76	86.85	-.03	1,959
88.74	85.86	Jun	86.81	86.81	86.87	-.03	954
88.53	85.66	Sep	86.91	86.80	86.91	.....	154
87.60	86.06	Dec	.....	.....	86.92	-.03	45

Est. sales 31,939. Prev. sales 26,270.
Prev day's open Int 37,457, off 360.

CATTLE, Live beef (CME)
40,000 lb.; ¢ per lb.

72.40	53.50	Apr	67.45	66.60	66.82	-.40	23,254
72.30	54.75	Jun	65.35	64.00	64.35	-.85	19,874
66.90	54.30	Aug	62.35	61.30	61.65	-.57	8,649
65.90	53.70	Oct	60.20	59.47	59.70	-.47	4,081
64.65	55.00	Dec	60.35	59.82	60.02	-.48	1,225
61.25	58.45	Feb	60.00	60.00	59.80	-.50	84
60.50	60.00	Apr	.....	.....	60.50	.....	9

Est. sales 19,274. Prev. sales 22,848.
Prev day's open Int 57,176, off 1,899.

SOYBEANS (CBT) 5,000 bu.; $ per bu.

9.08	5.94	Mar	6.16	5.91	6.16	+.21½	1,649
9.22	6.08½	May	6.29	6.05½	6.27½	+.18¼	32,807
8.66	6.18	Jul	6.36	6.15	6.35½	+.15¾	23,704
8.47	6.22	Aug	6.39½	6.18¼	6.38¼	+.15¾	2,893
7.77	6.22	Sep	6.39½	6.19	6.39½	+.16¼	1,696
7.79	6.27½	Nov	6.43	6.23½	6.41½	+.13¾	12,952
7.83½	6.39	Jan	6.54	6.36	6.53¾	+.12¾	1,921
7.44	6.53½	Mar	6.68½	6.49	6.68½	+.13	329
7.46	6.70	May	6.80	6.75	6.80	+.12½	18

Est. sales 46,803. Prev. sales 43,185.
Prev day's open Int 77,969, up 896.

Figure 9. Representative Commodity prices for March 15, 1982.
© 1982 by The New York Times Company. Reprinted by permission.

COFFEE "C" RULES

¶ 4501

Rule 8.00 (a) No Contract for the future delivery of Coffee "C" shall be recognized, acknowledged or enforced by the Exchange, or any committee or officer thereof, unless both parties thereto shall be members of the Exchange, provided, however, that members shall offer their contracts for clearance to the Clearing Association which shall become by substitution a party thereto in place of a member, and thereupon such Association shall become subject to the obligations thereof and entitled to all the rights and privileges of a member in holding, fulfilling or disposing thereof.

(b) THE FOLLOWING TEXT IS EFFECTIVE WITH RESPECT TO DELIVERY MONTHS UP TO AND INCLUDING MARCH 1982.

CONTRACT "C"
MILD COFFEE CONTRACT

New York _____ 19_____

(has)   (sold)
_____ (have) this day (bought)
(deliver to)

and agreed to receive from) _____ 37.500 lbs. of washed arabica COFFEE of the growths of Mexico, Salvador, Guatemala, Costa Rica, Nicaragua, Honduras, Colombia, Kenya, Tanzania, Uganda, New Guinea, Peru, Venezuela, Dominican Republic, Burundi, Ecuador, India, and Rwanda at the price of _____ cents per pound for growths of Mexico, Salvador, Guatemala, Costa Rica, Nicaragua, Kenya, Uganda or Tanzania, with additions or deductions for grades, and growths according to the differentials established by the Rules of the Exchange, adopted in accordance with the provisions of Coffee Trade Rule 8.00, and with additions or deletions for delivery points according to discounts and premiums as shall be established by the Board.

Delivery to be made from licensed warehouse in the Port of New York District, the Port of New Orleans or such other ports as may from time to time be added by the Board as authorized by the Rules of said Exchange, between the first and last day of _____, inclusive, the delivery within such time to be upon such notice to the buyer as may from time to time be prescribed in the Rules.

The delivery must consist of Coffee of one growth and must be in sound condition.

Coffee shall be sweet in the cup, good roasting quality, and of bean size and color in accordance with the description established by the Exchange. No delivery permitted of Coffee containing more than fifteen full imperfections below the basis, except that in the case of Colombian Coffee no delivery shall be permitted of Coffee containing more than ten full imperfections below the basis. Imperfections shall be established on the basis of a grading schedule established by the Exchange. Either party may call for margin as the variations of the market for like deliveries may warrant, which margin shall be kept good.

This contract is made in view of, and is in all respects subject to the Rules of the Exchange.

_____
(Brokers)

(Across the face is the following)

For and in consideration of One Dollar to _____ in hand paid, receipt whereof is hereby acknowledged _____ accept this contract with all its obligations and conditions.

Figure 10. (Courtesy of Coffee, Sugar and Cocoa Exchange Guide)

Commodity Calendar

Commodity Division			SEPTEMBER 1981	
Monday	**Tuesday**	**Wednesday**	**Thursday**	**Friday**
August 1981 S M T W T F S 1 2 3 4 5 6 7 8 9 10 11 12 13 14 15 16 17 18 19 20 21 22 23 24 25 26 27 28 29 30 31	**1** **Report:** Poultry Slaughter **First Notice Days/First Delivery Days:** Imp. Lean Beef, Palladium, Gold (IMM), Feeders, Rice (Rough, Milled), Citrus, Sugar #11, #2 Heating Oil, Oct. Broilers (CME)	**2** **First Delivery Day:** Rapeseed (WPG), 20 oz Gold (WPG)	**3**	**4** **Report:** Producer Price Index, **Report:** Employment/Unemployment
7 LABOR DAY EXCHANGES CLOSED	**8** October 1981 S M T W T F S 1 2 3 4 5 6 7 8 9 10 11 12 13 14 15 16 17 18 19 20 21 22 23 24 25 26 27 28 29 30 31	**9** **Last Trading Day:** GNMA-CD (CBT)	**10**	**11** **Reports:** CFTC Trader Commitments, USDA Crop Production, Retail Sales **First Notice Day:** GNMA-CD (CBT)
14 **Report:** USDA Ag Supply/Demand **Last Trading Day:** Currencies (IMM) **Report:** Inventories and Sales	**15** **Report:** USDA Cattle on Feed **Last Trading Day:** Lumber	**16** **First Delivery Days/First Notice Days:** Currencies (IMM), Lumber	**17** **Reports:** Housing Starts, Personal Income **Last Trading Day:** Citrus	**18** **Reports:** USDA Cold Storage, Capacity Utilization **Last Trading Day:** Feeders
21 **Reports:** Hogs & Pigs, USDA Soybean Stocks **Last Trading Day:** Plywood, Rapeseed (WPG), Soybeans, Oil & Meal, Grains (CBT), Coffee, Cocoa, Rough Rice, Milled Rice, GNMA-CDR, T-Bonds, T-Notes (4-6 yrs)	**22** **Report:** Eggs, Chickens & Turkeys **Report:** Durable Goods Orders	**23** **Last Trading Day:** T-Bills (IMM), Gold (IMM)	**24** **Reports:** Monthly Soy Crush, Consumer Price Index, USDA Livestock Slaughter **First Notice Day:** T-Bills (IMM), Oct. Cotton	**25** **Reports:** Citrus Fruits, Sugar Market Statistics **Last Trading Day:** Copper, Palladium, Imp. Lean Beef, Silver (Comex)
28 **Reports:** Monthly Ag Exports, Potatoes & Sweet Potatoes	**29** **First Notice Days/First Delivery Days:** 2 yr T-Note (Comex), Oct. Copper, Oct. Gold (Comex, CBT), Oct. Silver (Comex, CBT) **Last Trading Day:** T-Notes (2 yr - Comex)	**30** **Report:** Leading Indicators **Report:** USDA Ag Prices **First Notice Day:** Oct. Soybean Oil & Meal **Last Trading Day:** Oct. Sugar #11, Oct. 20 oz Gold (WPG), Oct. #2 Heating Oil	LAST TRADING DAYS — OCTOBER 1981 8 Cotton, Nov. Sugar # 1 20 Live Cattle, Feeders, Hogs 21 Soybean Oil & Meal 22 Broilers (CME)	LTDs — OCT. (Continued) 27 Copper, Silver (Comex, CBT), Gold (Comex, CBT), Platinum 30 Grains (WPG), Nov. Round Whites, Nov. #2 Heating Oil

Figure 11. (Courtesy of Commodity Research Bureau, Inc., New York, N.Y.)

COMMODITY CROSS REFERENCE

CITRUS
1 **First Notice Day:** Sep. Citrus
17 **Last Trading Day:** Sep. Citrus
18 **Report:** USDA Cold Storage
25 **Report:** Citrus Fruits
30 **Report:** USDA Ag Prices

COCOA
21 **Last Trading Day:** Sep. Cocoa

COFFEE
11 **Report:** USDA Crop Production
21 **Last Trading Day:** Sep. Coffee

COTTON
11 **Report:** USDA Crop Production
24 **First Notice Day:** Oct. Cotton

CURRENCIES
14 **Last Trading Day:** Sep. Currencies (IMM).
16 **First Notice Day:** Sep. Currencies (IMM)

FINANCIAL
4 **Report:** Employment/Unemployment
9 **Last Trading Day:** Sep. GNMA-CD (CBT)
11 **First Notice Day:** Sep. GNMA-CD (CBT)
    Report: Retail Sales
14 **Report:** Inventories and Sales
17 **Report:** Personal Income
18 **Report:** Capacity Utilization
21 **Last Trading Day:** GNMA-CDR
    Last Trading Day: Sep. T-Bonds
    Last Trading Day: Sep. T-Notes (4-6 yrs)
22 **Report:** Durable Goods Orders
23 **Last Trading Day:** Sep. T-Bills (IMM)
24 **First Notice Day:** Sep. T-Bills (IMM)
29 **First Notice Day:** Sep. 2 yr T-Note (Comex)
    Last Trading Day: Sep. 2 yr T-Note (Comex)
30 **Report:** Leading Indicators

FOREST PRODUCTS
15 **Last Trading Day:** Sep. Lumber
16 **First Notice Day:** Sep. Lumber
17 **Report:** Housing Starts
21 **Last Trading Day:** Sep. Plywood

FUEL OIL
1 **First Notice Day:** Sep. #2 Heating Oil
30 **Last Trading Day:** Oct. #2 Heating Oil

GRAINS
1 **First Notice Day:** Sep. Rice (Rough, Milled)
2 **First Delivery Day:** Sep. Rapeseed (WPG)
11 **Report:** USDA Crop Production
21 **Last Trading Day:** Sep. Rapeseed (WPG)
    Last Trading Day: Sep. Grains (CBT)
    Last Trading Day: Sep. Rice (Rough, Milled)

LIVESTOCK & MEATS
1 **First Delivery Day:** Sep. Imp. Lean Beef
    First Delivery Day: Sep. Feeders
15 **Report:** USDA Cattle on Feed
18 **Last Trading Day:** Sep. Feeders
21 **Report:** Hogs & Pigs
24 **Report:** USDA Livestock Slaughter
25 **Last Trading Day:** Sep. Imp. Lean Beef

METALS
1 **First Notice Day:** Sep. Palladium
    First Notice Day: Sep. Gold (IMM)
2 **First Delivery Day:** Sep. 20 oz Gold (WPG)
23 **Last Trading Day:** Sep. Gold (IMM)
25 **Last Trading Day:** Sep. Copper
    Last Trading Day: Sep. Palladium
    Last Trading Day: Sep. Silver (Comex)
29 **First Notice Day:** Oct. Copper
    First Notice Day: Oct. Gold (Comex, CBT)
    First Notice Day: Oct. Silver (Comex, CBT)
30 **Last Trading Day:** Oct. 20 oz Gold (WPG)

POULTRY
1 **Report:** Poultry Slaughter
    First Notice Day: Oct. Broilers (CME)
22 **Report:** Eggs, Chickens & Turkeys

POTATOES
11 **Report:** USDA Crop Production
28 **Report:** Potatoes & Sweet Potatoes
30 **Report:** USDA Ag Prices

SOYBEANS, OIL, & MEAL
11 **Report:** USDA Crop Production
21 **Report:** USDA Soybean Stocks
    Last Trading Day: Sep. Soybeans, Oil & Meal
24 **Report:** Monthly Soy Crush
30 **First Notice Day:** Oct. Soybean Oil & Meal

SUGAR
1 **First Notice Day:** Sep. Sugar #11
25 **Report:** Sugar Market Statistics
30 **Last Trading Day:** Oct. Sugar #11

OTHER REPORTS
4 Producer Price Index
11 CFTC Trader Commitments
14 USDA Ag Supply/Demand
24 Consumer Price Index
28 Monthly Ag Exports
30 USDA Ag Prices

WEEKLY REPORTS:

Monday — Export inspections for previous week
— grains and soybeans, hog/corn ratio
LME Warehouse Stocks
Tuesday — Weather and crops summary
USDA World Commodity Highlights
New York Cotton Weekly Open Interest
Wednesday — Broiler Production — 21 states
Cotton Loan Entries
Export inspections in previous week of
grains and soybeans to USSR and China
Thursday — Sugar Deliveries
Export Sales Commitments — grains,
soybeans related products and cotton
Weekly soybean crushings and capacity
FCOJ Movement figures
Friday — Bacon Slicings

Figure 12. **(Courtesy of Commodity Research Bureau, Inc., New York, N.Y.)**

and financial responsibility (meeting margin calls) for both seller and buyer.

Information on supply-demand statistics, technical patterns, and buy-sell recommendations can usually be had from the brokerage or independent advisories. Figures 11 and 12 depict some important dates for one month, including status reports and last trading days of many commodities.

Once the customer has opened the account, deposited monies, knows what he wants to trade, has information about the commodity, and has made up plans for trading, he will call his broker and place orders to transact trades.

TYPES OF ORDERS

A client can place several types of buy and sell orders. The principal ones are market, stop, and limit. A market order directs the floor broker on the exchange to execute the order promptly at the most favorable price possible. A limit order instructs the broker to buy or sell at a specified price, or better: a *sell* of December 1980 cattle at 70.50 would mean the broker must sell it at 70.50 or higher (say 70.55), while a *buy* at 70.50 would mean a purchase at 70.50 or lower (say 70.45). The buy stop order tells the broker to execute the order promptly as a market order when the price rises to and touches the specified price. A 70.50 buy stop for cattle would be executed immediately as a market order when the price rose from below 70.50 (say 70.30) to 70.50 or higher.

Other variations are used. An MIT order (market if touched) is something like the limit order but slightly different: it instructs the floor broker on a sell MIT order to sell the cattle contract when it hits 70.50, becoming, in effect, a market order, whereas the limit order specifies a price below which the transaction is unacceptable to the customer. Time orders can further delineate when the trade is to take place — a market on close means the order, a market execution, must be transacted at the close of business only. Other specialty orders include "FOK" (fill or kill — transact a specified limit order on the floor immediately or, if unable, cancel the order), and "TYT" (take your time — instructs the broker to fill it at the market, but perhaps not immediately, the exact timing being left to the discretion of the floor broker). Most of the orders are placed for execution for the day only, but open orders (good until cancelled) can be used, to be effective until executed or cancelled.

When an order is executed and the customer has bought a commodity contract, he will receive written and often verbal confirmation of the fact from his broker. It will show him on the date listed having bought or sold a given number of a specified commodity contracts at an executed price: "9/19/80 bought 2 Dec 80 Cattle 70.50."

Here it is appropriate to point out that because the client is trading a contract of cattle, say, and not the actual, cash item (40,000 lbs. in a pen in Chicago), he can arbitrarily be a buyer or the seller in the transaction. It is not necessary that he own the cows to contract to sell them, just as an automobile saleman may not have the car ordered by a customer actually on the car lot premises. Nor is it necessary for him to actually take delivery if he should be the buyer. He may take either side of the contract and at a later date take the other side. The computer in the exchange will offset the sale against the purchase and credit or debit the client (through the brokerage house) the difference in price, and no more obligation is left for the client. Only a few hedgers hold onto a bought or sold contract until the end of the contract, because they wish to take or make delivery.

STATEMENTS

If this is an initiation of a position, the statement will show only the confirmation of the execution; a line for cash balance, which is simply the deposit monies plus realized gains and losses to date less withdrawals plus additions of monies, and a line that tells the client the gain or loss on the open trade. For instance, if the client bought cattle on the day of the statement (or even before that) at 70.50 and the closing price at the end of the day was 70.70, the gain or loss would be current price less bought price times the gain (less if difference between prices is negative) per point times the number of contracts held. In this case, a gain of $(70.70 - 70.50) \times \$4$ per point $(.01) = \$80$ on the one contract. If there were other commodities held open at the same time, separate gains or losses for all positions would be listed.

The last entry, equity on position, plus cash balance, would be the total account equity.

Certain initial deposit or margin requirements are made for each commodity (for example, $1,500 for the above cattle contract) when the position is put on. Because the client is part of a contract, or promise, and does not physically own or have to sell the commodity in question at the time, only a "good faith" deposit, a fraction (usually 5–10%) of the value of what is traded, is required to write the contract. The deposit is needed to protect both client and broker against adverse price moves in the position, which is so highly leveraged. As long as there is excess money in the total equity column over and above that needed for all current position, it may be put on. Many brokerages allow the use of Treasury bills in another or the same account to count toward margins, but not toward losses (enough cash would have to be maintained for even slight losses). For example, if the client had three different commodity positions requiring $12,000 in margin and the total equity were $18,000, he would have an excess of $6,000 he could put into one or other new positions.

Brokerages also require that the total equity not get below a percentage (usually 75%) or fraction of the initial margin. In the above example, if the total initial margins were $12,000 for all positions, the brokerage would not allow the client to let his account slip below $9,000, or 75% of the original margin requirements. If it did and the client wished to not put in more money at that time, the maintenance call could be met by liquidating (closing out) positions and thereby reducing total initial margin requirements.

A confirmation closing a position will look like a statement of initiation, except that a realized profit or loss will show.

Most accounting systems are computerized — from the exchange to even the smallest brokerage house. The position (or part of it) will be closed when the initial trade side (say, bought) is offset by a later sale. If the client bought the cows for 70.50 and sometime later sold the same amount of cows for 70.80, the brokerage's computer will "match" buy and sale, compute the difference, and debit or credit the client after commissions and fees. Likewise, the reverse can occur: the client believing cow prices are going down in the future may sell at 71.20 and at a later date buy at a lower price (70.80). The computer would again match off the purchase against the sale, with only the sequence of dates showing differently; the sale came before the purchase. The importance is the "matching" or offsetting nature of buy and sell, not the sequence of events. The exchange acts as a clearing house by matching off and eliminating contracts that have our client as seller on some and buyer on others.

Many brokerages send out monthly statements, which summarize closed-out trades and list open trades, their open gain or loss, and initial and ending cash and total equity balances. These statements are particularly handy for tax time, when the capital gains form must show investments made.

TAX CONSIDERATIONS

According to former tax rulings, commodity trades lasting less than six months were treated as short-term capital gain or loss investments. Over six months qualified for long-term treatment.

As this chapter is being written, though, tax law on commodity trading is in a state of transition. According to the latest news from Capitol Hill, all commodity trades will be treated as short term and cumulative profits taxed at the end of each year, whether the trade has been closed out or is still open. But (good news to commodity traders) the tax rate would be a maximum of 32%, a vast improvement over the 70% maximum tax rate for the bulk of previous commodity trades. A $10,000 profit at the end of the year would mean only $3,200 would have to be given over to the government, if the investor were in the maximum tax bracket.

This feature makes it very attractive to trade commodities aggressively, for the investor can then keep the great bulk of hard-earned profits.

In the past, commodity customers have used spreads – the simultaneous buying and selling of the same or closely related commodity – to defer commodity or other short-term gains into the following year and/or convert them into long-term gains.

The one side of the spread (either purchase or sale) showing a loss the size of the short-term gain is closed out by the end of the year to establish an offsetting loss against the gain, hence no net gain or tax for the year. The gaining side is then carried into the next year. The risk of loss is reduced by immediately putting back on the side that was liquidated in the current year but a different contract month so that it doesn't become a useless wash. The long-term aspect comes into play if the losing side at the end of the current year is the sale of the commodity so that the purchase side is carried into the following year, for a total holding period of at least six months.

The IRS has questioned in the courts whether all this spending is just a bookkeeping operation with no capital risk at stake, and hence contends the operation constitutes a tax fraud. The defendants in such cases are contending that in many spread cases there is indeed some risk, and that spreading is a natural extension of the very short term nature of trading commodities. A third, and probably most compelling argument is, that if a trader is allowed to transact all sorts and lengths of time trades, this operation is merely a part of his overall risk-taking in commodities: if he has a nice gain, why should he have to choose between having to take it in a short interval, and risking *far* more than his original risk limitations by holding it for at least six months for a long-term gain?

Again, for the foreseeable future, it seems the latest congressional action setting a tax ceiling for trades of all time durations at 32% makes tax spreads rather useless.

CONCLUSION

In the investment rainbow, commodities trading constitutes a real viable alternative for not only beating the specter of inflation but making substantial capital gains. Commodity futures trading has a long history and a very substantial volume of business. Trading takes place in an auction environment in several concentrated areas — primarily in New York and Chicago in the United States. Accounts can be opened through firms with a network of nationwide offices, and business is transacted swiftly and simply.

What was not discussed and is very much absent in the commodity futures trading program is the trading plan. With all the electronic equipment, efficient marketplace, and accounting practices, a customer cannot make money without a good trading plan. The world's best computer cannot give good output without good data input or a well thought out program.

It is the intention of this book to investigate and develop a good trading plan for the investor.

4.
The Plan to Make Money

Like a cart without a horse (or even a horse without a cart), the profit potential without a good plan just will not make it. A carpenter requires tools to build a house or fashion furniture from materials. The investor needs timing and selection tools to make profits from financial opportunities.

Not just any tools will do. I have seen literally hundreds of methods and dozens of investment media that simply do not make money, or at best do so erratically. Also, I have researched and investigated many timing and selection approaches, and have found that they all have some good and some bad points. They all have weaknesses, some periods in time when they do not work well — there simply is no one "miracle method" which makes profits in all seasons. However, some are better than others, and a few are clearly superior to most.

The point of this book is to give the investor the maximum profit possible with an acceptable level of risk, by presenting the maximum leverage (highest return investment arena and best timing method) and strongest risk controls (diversification, reserve capital, and stop losses on trades) possible.

The chapter is split into three parts: the profit potential finder; the trade timer; and the management plan. These are the three "tools" that can translate investors dreams into profit reality: a plan that uses a profit selector and trade timer to not only make money beyond inflation's grip, but put the investor into the orbit of large wealth.

THE PROFIT FINDER

The profit potential finder is a selection routine that picks out commodities that over a long run should give more profit potential to our intrepid investor. It does not pick the commodity that will go up 165% from now to next May. Rather, it tells which ones are more *apt* to take off for greater profits than others.

Table 2 rates commodities by their historical profit size averages in uptrends and downtrends, separately. The first commodity in the uptrend ranking, gold, has an average move of 1.536 (or 153.6% move from its starting price) for every uptrend it has. That is, if the price started to move in an uptrend from a start of 100, gold would move 153.6 points, to 253.6, on the average. Another commodity, sugar, has an adjusted average (price fraction) of .684, so that it would move from 100 to 168.4, on the average, for its next uptrend. And so on.

Gold has the largest average move per uptrend, and so is ranked number one, followed by Treasury (T) bills, with the next highest, until the Canadian dollar, which has the smallest average move per uptrend.

The same logic can be used to arrange a downtrend ranking. The commodity that has the largest price-drop fraction on average is ranked number one. From Table 2 you can see that gold has an average move of 35.5% every time it drops into a downtrend, higher than the number five ranked commodity, coffee, which drops only 32.2% on the average when it starts into a downtrend.

These statistics were arrived at by averaging the sizes of uptrends, in fractions, for each commodity over approximately the past ten years, the accelerating inflation years. The same was done for downtrends for each commodity. (See "Trend Data" sections in my *Commodity Technical Yearbook.*)

These averages represent the average growth size, and hence potential for the future, in the face of continued and growing inflation. And should inflation temporarily subside, the downtrend averages represent the potential for *drops* in these commodities, and hence potential for making money on the *short* side.

I have taken into account the deposit or margin requirements in the average growths as an indicator of future profits. Margins, the money the investor puts up to trade a commodity and the basis for

Table 2.

Commodity	Uptrend Ranking	(Price Avg. Move (Fraction)
Gold	1	1.536
T-bills	2	.119*
Silver	3	1.188
Sugar #11	4	.684
Frozen orange juice	5	.673
Cotton	6	.652
Cocoa	7	.634
Swiss francs	8	.750+
Soybean meal	9	.593
Soybeans	10	.526
Coffee "C"	11	.522
Soybean oil	12	.495
Pork bellies	13	.464
Corn	14	.457
Wheat	15	.444
Copper	16	.419
W. German mark	17	.420+
Japanese yen	18	.417+
British pound	19	.412
Lumber	20	.395
Hogs	21	.392
Cattle	22	.369
T-bonds	23	.308
Ginnie Mae	24	.000
Canadian dollar	25	.000

Commodity	Downtrend Ranking	(Price Avg. Move (Fraction)
T-bills	1	.110*
T-bonds	2	.400+
Ginnie Mae	3	.400+
Gold	4	.355
Coffee "C"	5	.322
Soybean meal	6	.333
Sugar #11	7	.320
Swiss franc	8	.360+
W. German mark	9	.320+
Cotton	10	.291
Soybeans	11	.291
Pork bellies	12	.290
Frozen orange juice	13	.283
Soybean oil	14	.279
Cocoa	15	.264
Silver	16	.262
Hogs	17	.261
Corn	18	.261
Copper	19	.252
Wheat	20	.244
Japanese yen	21	.243
Cattle	22	.238
Lumber	23	.234
British pound	24	.250+
Canadian dollar	25	.150

*Equivalent to 1.190 or higher because of abnormally small margin requirements and high contract value.
+Diminished rank because of paucity of trend moves.

return on capital invested, are set by the exchanges and usually represent an average of 10% of the underlying price or value of the commodity.   The 10% figure changes sometimes from commodity to commodity and in volatile times is increased drastically. But these changes and fluctuations, like the market price moves, are random and average out to almost the same as a proportion of price for all commodities over a long period of time, and so fractional price change alone can be used as an indicator of return on capital, or profit, for the long run (which is what we care about).

In a way, the averages and the rankings represent the relative strengths of these commodities. We are looking for the commodities that grow the strongest in times of spiraling inflation, and the ones that drop the hardest in times of deflation or subsiding inflation. Robert Levy developed a relative strength concept and trading strategy for securities based on buying the highest ranked stocks in times of strong stock markets, and selling the lowest ranked ones in times of weakening markets.

While no guarantor of maximum future profits, the profit finder concept of relative strength is probably the best indicator of future profits.   One could argue that a thorough analysis of information fundamental to each commodity might indicate that cattle has the greatest potential move on the upside this year.

But there are many "ifs": if a harsh winter develops; *if* consumer demand for barbecues pick up hugely; *if* cattlemen truly cut back drastically on herd size; and so on.   I hold that it is next to impossible to predict ahead of time the size of a price move, because we simply don't know what events are going to transpire ahead of time (e.g., weather, demand, political, social, and economic events) with any great degree of certainty.

The best we can do is to pick best areas of growth based on historical growths on average, and assume that rankings based on those growth sizes will continue pretty much the same into the future, over a long number of growth periods.   That is, over the next ten or twenty uptrends gold makes over the years ahead, it will average higher growth moves than other commodities underneath it in the rankings.   The growth size averages may change, but the rankings should stay relatively the same.

THE PROFIT TIMER

Like love and marriage (or so it used to be), a profit selector and a timer go together like a horse and carriage. Gold may be the best single area to be in, but if one doesn't have a good timing device, not only won't he make much of the great profit potential, but he could lose money and lose badly because of the leverage and volatility of futures trading.

Timing trades is very important. It probably is the single most important tool, although again the investor could actually lose money if he didn't select a good commodity to follow (maybe he picked eggs in the spring, when nothing happens, so all trades made are losers), or didn't manage his money well enough (poor capital reserves knocked him out of the investment game after only one or two losses – oversized – depleted his capital to the nonplayable level).

The purpose of the timing method is to buy the commodity as cheaply and sell as expensively as possible; in a word, to be as efficient as possible in picking tops and bottoms in price moves.

I have examined many timing methods: forecasting, trend following, random market, pattern recognition, day trading – and many examples in each category.

Each method has advantages and disadvantages. Trend following methods are good in long, large-trending periods (obviously), but act poorly in choppy or sidewise price movements. Contrary methods act well in choppy, random (no direction) markets, but poorly in trended ones. Price forecasting sometimes works and sometimes does not.

Overall, one of the very best timing approaches is the moving-average method, and it is very easy to use. We will use it here.

MOVING AVERAGES

The moving-average approach is a popular one among "technical" practitioners in the stock and commodities markets. It is an easy one to formulate in quantitative terms and is less open to many interpretations than are other methods. It can be easily tested and manipulated on computers. For this reason, many serious analysts use this method to develop portfolio approaches to investing: computer-simulated track histories of a moving-average strategy can tell the analyst portfolio account values, growths, risks, and general market influences even on a day-to-day basis.

The assumption is that the moving-average line of current prices represents the current growth line of the trend. If the actual prices diverge significantly from this growth trend, such as to below the line in a bull trend or above the line in a bear trend, the current trend itself is then suspect, and a change in the actual prices to a new, oppositely directed trend has probably occurred.

The analogy with an assembly-line process is appropriate here. If too many of the sampled products on the assembly line (too much of the price series) are defective (violate the trendline), the conveyor belt and production process (current primary trend) are halted (trader closes out or reverses his position).

Figure 13 shows the essential use of the moving-average method. In example 1, a bull trend is in effect until the moving-average line *a* is intersected at price *A* by the actual prices. A bear trend is

1. Moving—average line *a* is violated when the actual prices cross the line at price *A* and signal a possible reversal in trend from bull to bear.

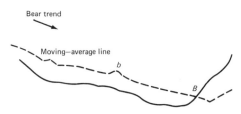

2. Moving—average line *b* is violated when the actual price series crosses the line at price *B* and signals a possible reversal in trend from bear to bull.

Figure 13. Basic idea of trend violation in the moving-average technique.

considered in effect from that point on. Example 2 is just the reverse of 1. A bear market is in effect until actual prices cross over and above the price B, indicating the probable birth of a bull trend.

HOW TO CALCULATE MOVING-AVERAGE DATA

Normally, moving-average data is calculated by adding together the past N days' closing prices and dividing by N.

The following formula is easier to calculate and is actually more general and sophisticated. The exponential moving average, S, for day i for the commodity under study is calculated as

$$S_i = A \times X_i + (1 - A) \times S_{i-1}$$

where A = weighting assigned to the latest closing price, and varies between 0 and 1 in value.

X_i = the closing price of the commodity under study for day i.

S_{i-1} = the exponential moving average for day i-1 (the day prior to day i).

and S_1 = X_1 (the first exponential moving average is equal to the first day's closing price)

Example

Suppose we are studying cattle closing prices. The following list of prices starts off at 10/02 and ends on 10/10 (the current date).

10/02	65.50	10/06	65.95
10/03	65.65	10/09	65.82
10/04	65.47	10/10	66.00
10/05	65.72		

Then $S_1 = X_1 = 6550$, the first price (on 10/02).
Now suppose we make $A = .1$, then

$$
\begin{aligned}
S_2 &= A \times X_2 + (1 - A) \times S_1 \\
&= .1 \times 65.65 + (1 - .1) \times 65.50 \\
&= 6.565 + (.9 \times 65.50) \\
&= 6.565 + 58.95 \\
&= 65.515
\end{aligned}
$$

Continuing,

$$
\begin{aligned}
S_3 &= A \times X_3 + (1 - A) \times S_2 \\
&= .1 \times 65.47 + (1 - .1) \times 65.515 \\
&= 6.547 + (.9 \times 65.515) \\
&= 6.547 + 58.9635 \\
&= 65.5105
\end{aligned}
$$

And

$$
\begin{aligned}
S_4 &= A \times X_4 + (1 - A) \times S_3 \\
&= .1 \times 65.72 + (.9 \times 65.5105) \\
&= 65.53145 \\
S_5 &= A \times X_5 + (1 - A) \times S_4 \\
&= .1 \times 65.95 + (.9 \times 65.53145) \\
&= 65.573305
\end{aligned}
$$

And so on.

Example

Suppose we have the following close price data for gold:

5/06	450.5
5/07	457
5/08	462
5/09	460
5/10	465

and we assign A to equal .2.
Then

$$
\begin{aligned}
S_1 &= X_1 = 450.5 \\
S_2 &= A \times X_2 + (1 - A) \times S_1 \\
&= .2 \times 457 + (1 - .2) \times 450.5 \\
&= 91.4 + 360.4 \\
&= 451.8
\end{aligned}
$$

And

$$S_3 = A \times X_3 + (1 - A) \times S_2$$
$$= .2 \times 462 + (.8 \times 451.8)$$
$$= 92.4 + 361.44$$
$$= 453.84$$

Continuing,

$$S_4 = A \times X_3 + (1 - A) \times S_3$$
$$= .2 \times 460 + (.8 \times 453.84)$$
$$= 92 + 363.072$$
$$= 455.072$$

Finally,

$$S_5 = A \times X_5 + (1 - A) \times S_4$$
$$= .2 \times 465 + (.8 \times 455.072)$$
$$= 93 + 364.0576$$
$$= 457.0576$$

Table 3 lists pertinent exponential moving-average information for the commodities listed. The smooth factor, A, is the same as explained in the calculations above, and represents a weighting on current data. If A is large (near to 1.0), then much emphasis in the formula is put on nearby (current) price data. A small value of A means that little emphasis is placed on current data, and more on past data (embodied in the second half of the formula, $(1 - A) \times S_{i-1}$). For example, $A = .5$ means the moving average is very sensitive to current data, dipping and rising very quickly. This value approximates a 3-day linear moving average (all three closing prices added, then divided by 3). For $A = .1$, this means the average is little dependent on current prices, and will rise or fall with current prices slowly (it approximates a 20-day linear moving average).

I have found 0.1 to be a good value for A for almost all commodities. It well represents the main trend in prices: it is not too sensitive nor too independent of current prices — any smaller and it would be insensitive to real, meaningful trend changes, and would

Table 3. Exponential Moving-Average Data.

Commodity	Smooth Factor (A)	Penetration Factor (P)	Stop Size Range
Cattle (live)	0.1	.03	.02 –.04
Cocoa	0.1	.05	.03 –.06
Coffee	0.1	.02	.01 –.06
Copper	0.1	.05	.01 –.02
Corn	0.1	.03	.03 –.06
Cotton	0.1	.05	.03 –.06
British pound	0.1	.003	.01 –.02
Canadian dollar	0.1	.003	.01 –.02
German mark	0.1	.003	.01 –.02
Japanese yen	0.1	.003	.01 –.02
Swiss franc	0.1	.003	.01 –.02
Gold	0.1	.05	.02 –.04
Ginnie Mae	0.1	.03	.03 –.06
Hogs	0.1	.03	.02 –.04
Lumber	0.1	.05	.03 –.06
Orange juice	0.1	.02	.01 –.02
Pork bellies	0.1	.05	.02 –.04
Silver	0.1	.05	.02 –.04
Soybeans	0.1	.05	.02 –.04
Soybean meal	0.1	.05	.03 –.06
Soybean oil	0.1	.05	.03 –.06
Sugar	0.1	.05	.03 –.06
T-bills	0.1	.003	.006–.012
T-bonds	0.1	.03	.03 –.06
Wheat	0.1	.03	.02 –.04

get the investor in too late on a trend, while any larger and it would make it too sensitive to day-to-day meaningless price change wiggling.

Through experience, I have found the values for the penetration factor and the stop size range indicated in Table 3 to be good.

THE PENETRATION FACTOR

The penetration factor (P) represents the price change fraction that current prices need to depart from the trend line (exponential moving-average calculation) to signal the start of a trend. For example, .05 value for p would mean gold prices would have to rise .05 or 5% above the current exponential moving-average calculation to signal an uptrend. If the exponential moving average were 500.00, then current closing price would need to rise to or above 500 + (.05 × 500) = 525 to signal the uptrend. A downtrend signal would be given if current prices fell below the exponential moving average by the factor amount: for the same average of 500, the current close price would have to fall to 500 – (.05 × 500) = 475 or below before the investor would be given a short signal.

THE STOP RANGE

The stop range (R) is expressed the same as the penetration factor (P) (in fractional terms) but represents an amount to add or subtract from the entry price of a position, to figure out a price to close out the new position taken in case the signal just given was just a false one (there really wasn't a change in trend).

For example, if the investor went long gold at 500.00 today, he might then set the stop to close out the position (in case the signal were a fluke and the long position was wrong) at 500 – (.03 × 500) = 485 sell stop, good until canceled (he cancels it when a signal in the opposite direction, sell short, occurs).

A short position would tell him to place a buy stop at 500 + (.03 × 500) = 515, good until canceled, for gold.

For long positions, then, the stop is placed the penetration factor amount times entry price, *below* the entry price, and left in until a sell short position is given. Likewise for short positions, the stop is placed at a price equal to the position entry price plus the penetration fraction times the entry price.

As indicated in the table, there is a *range* to pick from: the low number will be for more conservative investors, for which capital preservation is paramount — they are waiting to take many small losses waiting for the big profit: the larger number is for those who are more aggressive, have money to back up margin calls, and who don't want to get stopped out needlessly, for they don't want to miss the big, big move, which just might be this trade.

As I will mention in the management plan next, some investors will choose to use stops to protect against big losses and others will wait until reversing positions, and have no stops.

The moving-average timing method is a good technique to catch the start of a trend, but it also can get into "whipsaw" periods, in which small and moderate losses in succession occur because the formula gives false signals — little trends start but don't go anywhere, just far enough to get the investor into a new long or short position.

However, it is one of the few methods, and perhaps the only one, that almost assuredly gets the investor aboard the big trend moves when they do occur. I have argued that big trends (mostly uptrends) will occur in the future, due to inflation, and this is probably the best method to catch those trends. Also, the formula is very easy to compute — another added plus for the busy investor. The next section concentrates on how best to manage a portfolio to catch those profit moves and minimize losses intelligently.

TRADING HISTORY FOR THE FORMULA

The investor should check each commodity chapter following to see what the exponential moving average did in profits in past years. Some very good results for particular commodities are found there!

THE MANAGEMENT PLAN

The following discussions outline two ways the investor can use the profit finder (the commodity selection table) and the trade timer (the exponential moving average method) to make profits in the coming severe inflation/depression.

The first option is to use the formula strictly for timing trades in commodities chosen by the investor. He may wish to consult the chapters on individual commodities or other outside sources (government reports, his broker, etc.) to preselect the commodity.

The second option is a formal portfolio management plan, and is aimed at giving full guidance to the investor who is looking for long-term results.

Option No. 1: The Special Situation Plan

Some investors wish to be more aggressive, or more involved in each investment, or more independent of rigid plans, to take advantage of some special situation in investments that occasionally will command more of his attention and funds — with the objective of making much more money quickly.

The steps listed below will guide him in best utilizing the trade timer and commodity information in the following chapter to make big money in the coming inflation doom.

Step 1. Determine Which Commodities To Follow. The special situation investor will want to monitor a number of commodities to find that one or the few that have supertrend-making potential. He may decide, using information from his broker, general reading, or the chapters that follow, that gold is the prime supertrend mover for the year ahead. The potential finder, Table 1, may tell him to follow gold because it has incredible uptrends in inflationary times, much, much more than any other commodity. He is willing to forego other opportunities to wait for the one grand uptrend signal in gold. And he may be willing to invest a great proportion of his trading assets in gold, risking sizable loss if the uptrend signal turns out to be false, for the opportunity to make a fortune.

He should look for clues in each of the commodities discussed later on, to find that one or the few that can move considerably, and under what conditions. For example, commodities that have had high uptrend fractional moves (see each chapter) should continue to have large uptrends in inflationary spurts. Some collapse spectacularly in inflation setbacks or lull times, giving investors big opportunities for selling short. Check the downtrend fractional averages for each commodity.

Certain fundamentals of each commodity are tied in with inflationary binges. Cotton rises considerably when imported oil costs from OPEC rise even moderately, and even more so if there are weather droughts. Seasonal changes, government actions (crop reports, embargos, even election results) affect grains very much. Balance of payments trends greatly affect currency futures, and weekly money supply trends and Federal Reserve general credit policy most greatly affect interest rate futures.

Make sure to check the profit potential, fundamentals, and important events listed for each commodity with respect to high inflation in the chapters that follow.

Step 2. Use the Profit Timer Formula to Make Trades. Once the commodity has been chosen and is being monitored, the investor should use the profit (trade) timer, the exponential moving-average formula described before, to time entry and exit of positions.

Investors should pick a contract month that is quite active in trading (volume of sales and open interest are at least in the middle of all the months traded for that commodity), and preferably start following the commodity contract no more than six months before expiration, and get out of it before the first delivery notice day or the beginning of the last month of trading. Consult your broker for these details.

Start the formula for the first day of data collected, and continue per the formula instructions. Trades should be initiated when the current closing price exceeds the average S by at least the penetration fraction amount, $P,$ for long or purchase positions; or drops below the average S by at least the penetration fraction, $P,$ a short sell position. Of course, if the investor is only considering long positions, he should ignore the short sale signals, not go short but only close out his long position, and stand aside until a new long signal comes along.

The investor has the option of using or not using the stops, as explained in the formula section. For aggressive traders who have plenty of capital backing up the trade or will have more later on, he may not wish to use stops, lest he be stopped out needlessly and have the prices go in his favor subsequently. The more conservative trader will wish to use stops, to protect against large losses on each of these trades. He is essentially gunning for that big, big move, but wishes to sharply control his risk of loss on each attempt to pick a winner.

Option No. 2: The Formal Plan

The second option is designed for investors who wish to have a more methodical, automatic, longer-term plan for their monies. It is more formal and disciplined than the first option, and looks for large cumulative profits over a longer period of time, with little stress on getting a huge profit with a particular trade. There is also little judgment required on the part of the investor.

Initial Procedures. The investor must go through some easy steps to set up the portfolio and initiate trades. From that point on, only a

few minutes per day per commodity is required to do the calculations
and determine new positions and current portfolio status.

Step 1. Determine Capital Commitment. The investor must decide
how much money he can afford to put into the portfolio. He will
need a minimum of $10,000 to cover the cost of diversifying over
just a few commodities and keeping ample reserves. The larger the
commitment, the better off he will be! He'll be able to diversify
more, which reduces risks, keep bigger reserves, which also reduces
risk by helping to nullify sequences of losses, which sometimes
occur, and capture more trends, even perhaps all the big ones, which
improves cumulative profits, when he is able to diversify more.

Step 2. Determine the Reserve Amounts. If he is conservative (no
more monies to add to the portfolio, or he wishes to see no more
than 50% paper loss at any point), then he will keep 70% in reserve.
More aggressive traders will set 50% or even 30% reserves.

For a $10,000 account, this means a conservative fellow would
keep $7,000 in reserve and only $3,000 put up for commodity
margins. An aggressive sort would put, say, $5,000 in reserve and
$5,000 in commodities, or perhaps only $3,000 in reserve and
$7,000 in commodities.

For a $100,000 account, the conservative investor would have
only $30,000 in commodities, the balance in reserve.

Step 3. Determine No. Commodities in Portfolio. Given the reserve
amounts and the amount to be allocated to commodities, the investor
can then divide the commodity amount by the average margin in
dollars over all commodities to find out approximately how many
commodities he can have simultaneously in the portfolio.

For example, if he keeps only $3,000 in commodities and the
average margin is $1,500 then he can only follow $3,000/$1,500 = 2
commodities. A $100,000 account with the same proportion (70%)
could have $30,000/$1,500 = 20 commodities in his portfolio at
one time.

Of course, not all commodities have the same margins. In fact,
they are mostly different. It is best to put equal *dollars* commited to
each commodity (from the standpoint of risk minimization). For

example, one corn contract currently has approximately one-third the margin of a soybean contract, so we would normally put three contracts of corn in the portfolio for every one of soybeans.

Step 4. Determine Which Commodities to Monitor. This is a personal matter, and related to the investor's capability and preference to follow as many commodities as he can. Some will prefer to follow just one of each major group (e.g., a metal, meat, grain, sweet, currency, fiber, and a financial future), while others may want to follow all commodities or just several groups. I would advise the investor to spread out as much as possible, to reduce the risk and enlarge the potential for grabbing on to a big trend or two to cumulate more profits for the portfolio. Even if he follows all major commodities, that amounts to around twenty, not a burdensome number.

Step 5. Set Up the Calculations. For each commodity followed, there should be a page with a column for date, another for current closing price, and one for the new exponential moving average (S) using that current closing price (see "How to Calculate the Moving Average"). The investor should place the formula on the top of the page to refer to. A column labeled "Action" will complete the tabulations necessary. (See sample page, Figure 14.)

A separate page should list current positions: how many contracts, the commodity, its position (long or short), margin is tied up, its stop price, and the average move (price fraction) for the commodity's uptrend (long position) or downtrend (short position). (See "The Profit Finder" for explanations of the average move.) Figure 15 is an example of the current position sheet.

$$S_i = .1 \times X + .9 \times S_{i-1}$$

Commodity	Date	Closing Price	S	Action
Wheat, Dec. 1981	9/15/81	425.5	422.26	
	9/16/81	425.0	422.76	
	9/17/81	423	422.79	
	9/18/81	435	424.01	Go Long:
	9/21/81	429	424.51	
	9/22/81	430	425.06	

Figure 14. Commodity Position Table.

Maximum Position = 5

Qty	Commodity	Pos.	Margin	Stop Price	(Price Ave. Move (Fraction)
2	Wheat, Dec. 1981	Long	$2,400	417 sell	.425
2	Cattle, Dec. 1981	Long	2,000	6550 sell	.363
1	Gold, Dec. 1981	Short	2,000	480 buy	.551
	TOTALS		$6,400		

Figure 15. Current Positions.

Step 6. Start the Calculations. Collect enough closing price data (one full month should do it) for each commodity and record it on the position sheet for each one (along with the data). Starting with the first date, calculate the exponential moving average (S), as per the instructions in "How to Calculate the Moving Average," using the smooth factor (A) from Table 3 in the formula. After completing the calculations through the present (including today), go back and see if there are any uptrend or downtrend signals. Using the penetration factor (P) from Table 3 for each commodity, see if current prices *today* are above or below the moving coverage (S) for *yesterday* by the penetration fraction times the moving average. Refer to "The Penetration Factor" in the preceding section for examples. In the Commodity Position sheet in Figure 14, for example, the closing price for Dec. 1981 wheat on 9/18 (435) was higher than the moving average of 9/17 (422.79) by more than the penetrating factor (.03, or 3%, for wheat — Table 3), and so a "Go long" signal was recorded.

If there is an uptrend signal, the message "Go long" is marked in the "Action" column, and if a downtrend signal occurs, the notation should be "Go short." It is possible that both signals could happen in the time period covered (but not the same day), so don't be confused. Mark down all trend signals.

Step 7. Initiate Positions. Once the investor has gotten up to date on calculating and figuring out the most current positions for all the commodities followed and he has his money ready, the fun begins.

He should only initiate positions on the opening the day following the signal, and only then. This means he may have to wait some time for new signals to come along before he can actually participate.

Positions (long or short) are taken until all available slots for investment monies are taken up. That is, from Step 3 ("Determine No. Commodities in Portfolio"), he knows the maximum number of commodities in the portfolio at any one time (mark that number on the top of the current position sheet). If the maximum were five, for example, he would take new positions until he had five different commodity positions, and no more.

If he uses no stops at all, the initial group chosen for positions will be the *only* group ever traded since he will merely be reversing positions. In that case, he should choose carefully to initiate only those he wishes to be in the portfolio.

Note also from Step 3 that the numbers of contracts for each commodity will vary, depending upon the margin requirements for each. The rule is, equal *dollars* (approximately) to each position. Hence two contracts of wheat are about the same (in profit, risk, and dollars potential) as two contracts of cattle, but only one of gold.

If the trader is using stops, he should record the fact to the side of the "Action" column on each commodity position sheet, or the current position sheet where actual trades are in progress. Refer to "The Stop Range" to see how to use it in practice.

Step 8. Everyday Procedures. Once the initial procedures of setting up calculation and position sheets and actual positions have been taken up to the maximum allowed, then daily tracking and adjustments of positions can begin. The following tells how to routinely manage the active portfolio. For each day;

1. *Continue calculating moving averages (S) for each commodity.* (See "How to Calculate the Moving Average.") If the commodity in question has come to the month of its expiration, then change over to another contract month no more than six months away or less than two months. In such a case, repeat the instructions, Step 5, "Start the Calculations." If the new contract month shows the same position as of today, then simply close out the old position (if held in the portfolio) and open up the same position with the new contract. If not, wait for a new signal to contemplate initiating a new position.

2. *Check if any actual current positions have been stopped out.* If your broker informs you that you have been stopped out of one or more positions, cross them off the current position sheet and keep a mental note of how many positions are now freed up for new commodity trades.

3. *Check if new signals have been generated.* If new signals have been generated, have those positions initiated at the next morning's opening with stops entered if desired (see "Initial Positions" and "The Stop Range" for proper calculations) *if* they fulfill one of the following criteria:

   a. *For long signals.* If the new signal is a long position or up-trend signal, then initiate the new trade if there is an open slot available, or if the new commodity's uptrend move size is larger than the uptrend move size for a current *long* position, or larger than the downtrend move size of a current *short* position. Close out the old position at the opening tomorrow. Refer to Table 2 in "The Profit Finder" section to check sizes and uses of the move sizes.

   As an example, if the new signal were for an uptrend in orange juice, the investor would see if any slots were free for new trades. If not, then its uptrend move size (say, .673) would be checked against the uptrend move sizes of current long positions first. If none were lower, then the same figure (.673) would be checked against the downtrend move size averages of current *short* positions. Usually the uptrend sizes are bigger than downtrend ones, so this one should be longer than one of the short's downtrend move size averages. If he were currently short corn, say, and if corn had a down-trend move size average of .322, then the orange juice long would replace the corn short because its uptrend size .673 (associated with the long position) was larger than the downtrend size of corn, .322 (associated with its short position), and represented a larger potential profit.

   The purpose of this replacement of positions is to be always in the commodity with the largest move potential, up or down, to enable the trader to capture *larger* potential profits.

   b. *For short signals.* If the new signal is a short position, or downtrend signal, then initiate the new trade if there is an open slot available now or if the new commodity's downtrend move size average is larger than the uptrend move size for a current *long* position, or larger than the downtrend move of a current *short* position. Close out the old position(s) at the opening tomorrow. Again, refer to Table 2 to find the appropriate sizes for the move averages.

For example, if the new signal were a short in gold, and all slots were filled with positions, then its downtrend average move size (say, .436) would be first checked against move sizes of current long positions. If all were larger then .436, then downtrend move size averages of current short positions would be scrutinized to see if there were any that were smaller than .436. If there was one (say cattle, at .332), the cattle short position would be closed out and the gold position initiated the next morning at the opening.

5.
Trading Results Explained

The following explanations and example show how to interpret trading result tables found in each of the chapters on individual commodities.

DATA AND HEADINGS

The listing below describes and explains the data headings for the trading results tables in the following chapters. Refer to Table 4 for examples of the headings.

1. *Contract.* The month, year, and future tested are listed. In Table 4, May 1980 soybean meal is to be tested.
2. *Parameter.* Parameter settings for the moving-average method are listed in this column. For implications and understandings of the use of parameter values, refer to Chapter Four. Parameter A is the smooth factor and P is the penetration fraction. In Table 4, the example is $A = .1$ and $P = .05$ for soybean meal.
3. *Position.* Positions long (+) or short (−) for the method are delineated in this column. The first position in the Table 4 example is +, or a long position.
4. *Date in.* Calendar date is listed for entry of the position taken. The first trade in Table 4 was initiated on June 8, 1979.
5. *Price in.* The price taken for the position shown is listed here, and is equal to the closing price for that day. In Table 4, the first trade was initiated at 214.50.

Table 4. Sample Trading Results.

MOVING AVERAGE METHOD

CONTRACT PARAMETERS	POS	DATE IN	PRICE IN	DATE OUT	PRICE OUT	GAIN(LOSS)	MAX LOSS	OPEN DATE
SOYBEAN MEAL MAY 1980 A P .100 .050								
	+1	60879	214.50	62979	202.50	-12.00	12.5	62979
	-1	62979	202.50	52080	168.00	+34.50	18.5	70979
TOTAL						+22.50		
AVE.GAIN	34.5	AVE.LOSS	12.0					
RATIO G/L	2.8	SUCCESS RATE	0.50	NO. TRADES	2			

POINTS-TO-DOLLARS CONVERSION TABLE

Commodity	Points in Tables	=	Dollars
Cattle (live)	1.0		$ 4.00
Cocoa	1.0		3.00 for 1980 10.00 for 1981
Coffee	1.0		3.75
Copper (N.Y.)	1.0		2.50
Corn	1.0		50.00
Cotton	1.0		5.00
Currencies			
British pound	1.0		2.50
Canadian dollar	1.0		10.00
Deutsche mark	1.0		12.50
Japanese yen	1.0		12.50
Swiss franc	1.0		12.50
Ginnie Mae	1.0		31.25
Gold	1.0		100.00
Hots (live)	1.0		3.00
Lumber	1.0		100.00
Orange juice	1.0		1.50
Porkbellies	1.0		3.80
Silver	1.0		50.00
Soybeans	1.0		50.00
Soybean meal	1.0		100.00
Soybean oil	1.0		6.00
Sugar #11	1.0		11.20
Treasury bills	1.0		25.00
Treasury bonds	1.0		31.25
Wheat	1.0		50.00

6. *Date out.* The calendar date for exit (closing) of the position is listed in this column. For the example in Table 4, the date out is June 29, 1979, for the first trade.

7. *Price out.* The price at which the position was closed is shown here, and is equal to the closing price for that day. For the first trade in Table 4, the exit price is 202.50.

8. *Gain (Loss).* The gain (+) or loss (–) in points, and excluding commissions, is listed in this column. For conversion to dollar gain or loss, refer to the points-to-dollar conversion table. Commissions and margins are not shown or figured in because they vary with each brokerage house. The first trend in Table 4 was closed out with a loss of 12.00 points.

9. *Max loss.* The largest (paper) loss incurred before the current position is closed out. The worst (paper) loss before the first trade was completed in Table 4 was 12.5.

10. *Open date.* The date on which the largest (paper) loss of the current position occurred before it is closed out. The date for the worst open loss for the first trade in Table 4 was actually June 29, 1979, the day the position was subsequently exited (on the close).

11. *Total.* Total gain or loss in points is listed for the period covered. The sum of all trades (2) in Table 4 was 22.50 profit, the result of a loss (–12) and a gain (+34.50).

12. *Average gain.* The simple arithmetic average of all gains derived for the particular parameter setting of the method under consideration is listed. In Table 4 there was only one gain, so the average is the same, or 34.50.

13. *Average loss.* The simple arithmetic average of all losses shown for the parameter setting of the method under consideration is listed. The average loss was the same as the single loss, or 12.0, in the Table 4 example.

14. *Ratio G/L.* The ratio G/L (gain to loss) is computed as the magnitude of the average gain divided by the average loss. The average gain (34.5) divided by the average loss (12.0) yielded a return of 2.8 for the trades in Table 4.

15. *Success rate.* The success rate (a fraction) is calculated as the total number of gaining trades divided by the total number of gaining and losing trades for the parameter setting and method listed. In Table 4, there was one gain trade out of two total trades, so the success rate was ½ = 50%.

6.
Cattle Profits

Live cattle futures are traded on the Chicago mercantile exchange and enjoy a good, brisk, trading volume, approaching as much as 40,000 contracts a day. The trade is evenly balanced between speculators and hedgers, with perhaps a tip toward hedging. Gains and losses run as high as $600 per contract per day, a moderate amount. Table 1 in Chapter Three lists the details of the contract. Each cent price move per contract is equivalent to $400, and each 5-cent price move is equivalent to $2,000.

THE PROFIT POTENTIAL

Cattle has gone through two stages of price development. From its trading inception in 1964 until 1973, trends were very small and price changes gradual. It was a good commodity for beginners to learn to trade. With the onslaught of the Russian wheat deal, drought and inflation in 1973–4, prices movements quickened. A long up-trend began in late 1970 and peaked in 1973 at 60 cents per pound – a move from beginning to end of over 30 cents, or $12,000 profit on the long side for patient traders putting up only $900 in margin. Prices have greatly vascillated since, bouncing between the high 30s and 80 cents, with a few 20-cent moves, two 25-cent moves, and one thirty-cent move interspersed. (See Figure 16 for a graph of cattle prices throughout its history.)

The price structure has been moving upward over the years, in a stepwise fashion. This overall upward tendency reflects growing population, feed costs, and interest rates. As with most grains (on

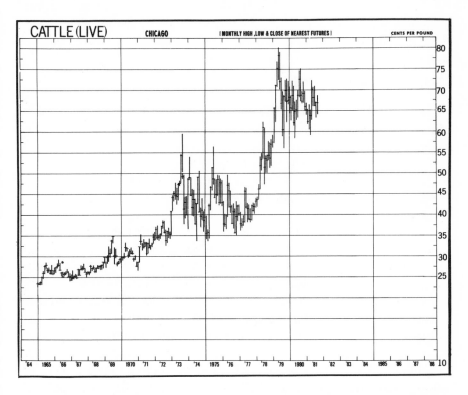

Figure 16. Cattle (monthly chart). (Courtesy of Commodity Research Bureau, Inc., New York, N.Y.)

which it depends for feed, and because feed is a main-cost ingredient, its price is often strongly dependent on the grains), cattle prices move up strongly in a short period (one or two years), then sit sideways for three or four years, while its cycles and other costs dampen prices.

We are currently nearing the end of one of those sideways, or plateau, stages. The next move should be on the upside, for a sharp move of 30–40 cents.

From Table 2, Chapter Three, cattle has a relatively low uptrend ranking (22) because of its .369 average price fraction move on the upside. This means it will move .369 × 60 = 22 cents from its last base of 60 cents. The profit potential of 22 cents means around $9,000 on about $1,000 average current margins, still a good return.

The downtrend, or short sell, potential is .238, or around 14 cents at the 60-cent level, or $6,000.

THE FUNDAMENTALS

The cattle industry is big. The U.S. raises about 10% of the world's beef, and this well exceeds 100 million head. The income from cattle raising is more than most grains and fiber combined, and feed for cattle comprises the single largest use of feed grains.

Cattle take long to raise. Hence, changes in herd supply are long and gradual. Raising a calf to marketable weight takes two to three years.

Demand for beef depends on the size of the human population, purchasing power, price of competitive products like hogs, lamb, and poultry, government purchases, and public taste. It stays relatively constant compared to supply in the short run.

Supplies depend upon the size of the population of calves and mature animal on-feed. The weight (like yield in grains) and hence size of supplies depend upon cost of feed and condition of the grazing land.

Droughts and freezes affect immediate and sometimes long-run supplies. They often force cattlemen to bring animals not quite ready to market, building supplies up temporarily and reducing the next term's supplies and quality of cow, making supplies and price often erratic.

Exports and imports are of little influence on cattle supplies or demand.

There are two major cycles that bear on long-term price patterns: the long-term birth-slaughter cycle and the seasonal periodicity.

The birth-to-slaughter cycle comes out of the long breeding to maturity of the animal: it takes three years, partly on the range and the last year to year and a half in feedlots, to raise the calf to slaughter weight. This accounts for the farmer influencing, by his heavy or light marketings at times, the basic trends in prices. In the basic cycle, the first phase consists of the farmer deciding to expand his stock in response to the anticipation of rising prices. The second phase means further withholding of animals as prices do indeed increase, which action further increases prices. In the third phase, an impasse is reached: the expanded herd must come to market (it is ready to be fattened). This increases slaughter and supplies, and prices begin to falter and slide. The fourth phase is an acceleration of the third phase: the farmer starts to market more and more of his steer as prices fall more and more (he is afraid of being stuck with excess herd and no effective marketing or good prices available). The cycle lasts anywhere from a few years to ten years, but normally around four years.

The seasonal cycle has to do with cattle-breeding habits. Most calves are born within 40–45 days of April 1, wintered on western ranges for about six months, summered for another six months on the Great Plains, and then sent to feedlots for the final 200 days or so. The rate of slaughter has a slight tendency to rise in October and dip in February.

IMPORTANT EVENTS TO LOOK FOR – AND THEIR EFFECTS

1. *Cattle on feed reports.* Quarterly reports by the Department of Agriculture in mid-March, June, September, and December. The important thing to check for is the difference between pre-report guesstimates by traders and hedgers and the actual report. A shocking, unexpected report often starts big trends.
2. *Four-year cattle cycle.* Described above. Look for large changes in marketings – up or down – to indicate the start or peak of the major cycle.
3. *Competitive products and other reports.* The cold-storage report, showing belly stocks, and the hogs report influence cattle prices, sometimes greatly. Likewise, monthly grain crop reports, especially in drought times, affect the cost of cattle feed (the grains), and hence cattle prices tend to follow grain prices and events.
4. *Weather events.* Freezes and droughts in cattle territory affect, for the short term, prices upwards.

THE RECORD: 1980-1

Parameters for the moving-average method applied to cattle are listed in Table 3, Chapter Four.

Table 5.

MOVING AVERAGE METHOD

CONTRACT PARAMETERS	POS	DATE IN	PRICE IN	DATE OUT	PRICE OUT	GAIN(LOSS)	MAX LOSS	OPEN DATE
CATTLE								
JUNE 1980								
A P								
.100 .030								
	+1	61179	7200.00	72679	6910.00	−290.00	290.0	72679
	−1	72679	6910.00	81479	7082.50	−172.50	200.0	81479
	+1	81479	7082.50	10880	7157.50	+75.00	245.0	82179
	−1	10880	7157.50	20680	7420.00	−262.50	312.5	20680
	+1	20680	7420.00	31780	6925.00	−495.00	510.0	31780
	−1	31780	6925.00	50980	6717.50	+207.50	120.0	31980
	+1	50980	6717.50	62080	6902.50	+185.00	382.5	60380

TOTAL   −752.50
AVE.GAIN   155.8 AVE.LOSS   305.0
RATIO G/L   0.5 SUCCESS RATE 0.42 NO. TRADES   7

CONTRACT PARAMETERS	POS	DATE IN	PRICE IN	DATE OUT	PRICE OUT	GAIN(LOSS)	MAX LOSS	OPEN DATE
JUNE 1981								
A P								
.100 .030								
	+1	72380	7510.00	120980	7240.00	−270.00	330.0	82580
	−1	120980	7240.00	33181	6855.00	+385.00	85.0	122280
	+1	33181	6855.00	51281	6775.00	−80.00	105.0	40381
	−1	51281	6775.00	52981	6817.50	−42.50	97.5	52881

TOTAL   −7.50
AVE.GAIN   385.0 AVE.LOSS   130.8
RATIO G/L   2.9 SUCCESS RATE 0.25 NO. TRADES   4

The two years covered were rather unspectacular with regard to trends: in 1980, although prices ranged from 62 to 76 cents, enough for ample profits if only one or two trends ran from one extreme to the other, it was not a good year for trend methods, as prices vacillated tightly, for the most part in the middle of the range, from 68 to 72. That range was enough to trigger buy and sell signals, but not smoothly changing enough to produce regular profits, and so overall losses were recorded with the moving-average method (about 7.5 cents, or $3,000). Stops would have reduced losses by several cents but not eliminated them. Nineteen eighty-one contract trades showed nearly break-even results, with gains of 1.5 cents if stops had been instituted. (Refer to Table 5 for the details for both years' trading results, and to Chapter 5 for details on how to read the table.)

IN THE FUTURE

Cattle futures prices have always moved slowly, almost deliberately. Very long trends have occurred nearly every year, ranging from 10 cents to 30 cents. Most trend-following methods have done well in these markets. The current stagnation is due to change soon, with several long trends forecast.

7.
Cocoa Profits

Cocoa futures are traded both in London and New York. The discussion below will pertain to New York operations. Trading has been moderate, averaging a few thousand contracts a day. The balance of trading is heavily weighted toward hedgers, such as confectioners, general food companies, and candy manufacturers. Each dollar price move per tonne is equal to $10 for each contract, and a $500 move per tonne is equivalent to $5,000.

THE PROFIT POTENTIAL

Cocoa has been attractive to speculators because it has tended to have long, extensive trends (see "Fundamentals" for reasons). Even as far back as the early fifties, it had moves of 100% and 200% of price that were long lasting and had low margins (see Figure 17 for long-term price moves history). There was a period of dormancy in most of the sixties, followed by some long uptrends starting in 1965, and again in 1972 and 1975. The last two trends were especially large, amounting to 300% and 400% increases in price over two years. These moves were due to general inflation and sympathy with other foodstuffs in the 1972 rise, and supply scarcity due to drought and other factors in the 1975 move.

Since that time, a long downtrend of almost 80% over four years occurred (with a few small uptrends as interruptions), again showing the long-term potential. Margins have been relatively low, about 5%

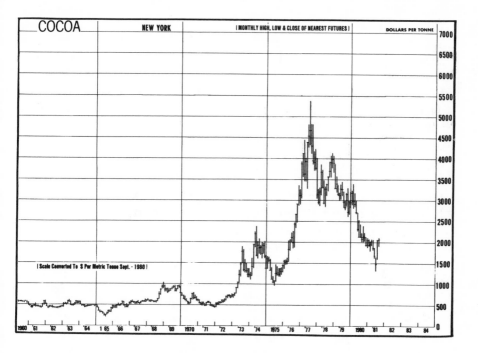

Figure 17. "Cocoa"—monthly futures price. (Courtesy of Commodity Research Bureau, Inc., New York, N.Y.)

of price in most times, so profits could have ranged to as high as 8,000% on the 1975 move!

The brown bean has ranked high (#7) in uptrend moves among all commodities in the past ten years, with a mediocre performance in downtrend ranking (#15). Except for recent stellar performances by gold, silver and T-bills, cocoa has ranked near the very next highest, with a .634 average uptrend move fraction. This means a 63.4 unit move from a 100 base for the average uptrend — or about 12 times the normal margin requirement of 5 units — plenty of room for a large average profit on the long side.

Cocoa has had a long downtrend and is probably ready for not only a large uptrend, but a series of them, similar to the two major and minor moves from 1972 on.

FUNDAMENTALS

In the short run, demand and supply for cocoa are relatively inelastic. Supply stays relatively stable because of the amount of time it takes to bring new trees to maturity (4 to 5 years). Demand does not change radically in a short spell either, because commercial users find substitutes for the oils, change their product chocolate consistency, or simply pay higher prices (labor, distribution and manufacturing costs are a higher proportion of a typical candy product).

From time to time, cocoa producers ban together to try to set (dictate) prices, but these alliances always seem to fall apart — no one seems to trust the other, and users find some way to lower consumption. Hence, the producers get stuck with large surpluses on their hands.

The main producers are Ghana, Nigeria, Brazil, Ivory Coast, Cameroon, and Toga, which account for around 80% of the world's cocoa production.

The crop year runs from October through September, with about 80% of the crop harvested in the first six months. Crop estimates are given by the producing countries, in the form of government purchases from the farmers, but these are considered to be notoriously unreliable (often they form the front end of government policy, to artificially boost prices up).

It has been asserted that the elasticity of demand for cocoa is about 0.25: if cocoa production falls off by 25%, prices will rise by 100%. This explains long price rises, certainly.

Seasonality also plays a part. Like the grains, there tend to be heavy marketings and pressure on prices starting in October, but lasting through the early winter. In our summer, the needs of commercial users for the fall and winter create upward pressure on price.

IMPORTANT EVENTS TO LOOK FOR —
AND THEIR EFFECTS

1. Weekly main-crop purchases by the market boards of Ghana and Nigeria, beginning in October. These can (even falsely) start or accelerate a trend in progress.
2. Census Bureau monthly reports covering United States Confectionery Store Reports on sales of chocolate items. This helps indicate increases or decreases in demand.

3. New York Cocoa Exchange reports on cocoa stocks. This affects the total supply available to users.
4. U.N. Food and Agriculture Organization, and Producers Alliance periodic production forecasts.
5. Gill and Duffus supply and demand statistics (especially grindings). Probably the most timely and accurate of the reports.

THE RECORD: 1980-1

Parameters for the moving-average method applied to cocoa are listed in Table 3, Chapter Four. The two years chosen for tests of the method were for the most part major downtrends. In fact, of the four short sales taken (see Table 6), only one was a loser, while the other three yielded good size gains. All long positions were losers — the main

Table 6.

MOVING AVERAGE METHOD

CONTRACT PARAMETERS	POS	DATE IN	PRICE IN	DATE OUT	PRICE OUT	GAIN(LOSS)	MAX LOSS	OPEN DATE
COCOA MAY 1980 A .100 P .050								
	−1	101579	13510.00	112679	14050.00	−540.00	540.0	112679
	+1	112679	14050.00	22180	13630.00	−420.00	730.0	10280
	−1	22180	13630.00	52080	11010.00	+2620.00	770.0	32480

TOTAL   +1660.00
AVE.GAIN 2620.0 AVE.LOSS 480.0
RATIO G/L 5.4 SUCCESS RATE 0.33 NO. TRADES 3

CONTRACT PARAMETERS	POS	DATE IN	PRICE IN	DATE OUT	PRICE OUT	GAIN(LOSS)	MAX LOSS	OPEN DATE
MAY 1981 A .100 P .050								
	−1	52080	2569.00	91280	2455.00	+114.00	116.0	60680
	+1	91280	2455.00	92980	2250.00	−205.00	210.0	92980
	−1	92980	2250.00	43081	1865.00	+385.00	98.0	100980

TOTAL   +294.00
AVE.GAIN 249.5 AVE.LOSS 205.0
RATIO G/L 1.2 SUCCESS RATE 0.66 NO. TRADES 3

trend simply was down, and there wasn't enough room for profits in the short duration and move of the brief uptrends. All in all, the method performed well over the two years, returning about 200% net profits on margin deposits each year. (Refer to Chapter 5 for details on how to read Table 6.)

IN THE FUTURE

Cocoa futures reflect general inflation like a mirror, and have extended moves. The current set of trends has been overwhelmingly on the downside. Both returning inflation and the oversold present condition should propel prices strongly upward in the near future.

8.
Coffee Profits

Coffee futures are traded in New York and London. The New York exchange will be the subject of this chapter. Trading enthusiasm has varied, from moderate to heavy volume. It is heavily dependent on weather and cartel operations, but currently averages a few thousand contracts a day, and is evenly split between hedging and speculator interests. Each cent price move is equivalent to $375 per contract, and each twenty-cent move is equivalent to $7,500.

THE PROFIT POTENTIAL

Coffee has had a roller-coaster history of price moves and trading participation. In the 1950s and 60s, trading volume was dormant and price moves were sedate (except for 1954 when a severe frost hit and prices soared vertically). Partly as a result of inflation in 1973 and 1974, coffee prices became more active. Twice in the past six years, devastating freezes have skyrocketed prices, with good downtrends intervening. The first uptrend, in 1975 (see Figure 18) catapulted nearly 600% in price, from 50 cents to nearly $3.50 per pound (most housewives remember the great supermarket hike). The move amounted to over $100,000 in gains on the long side, with margins initially around $1,500, for a whopping gain of 6,000%! Currently, prices are quite depressed, in the $1.00–1.50 per pound range.

Coffee makes long trends, but with great volatility about the growth line.

Figure 18. Coffee "C"—monthly chart prices. (Courtesy of Commodity Research Bureau, Inc., New York, N.Y.)

The addictive drink has a good average uptrend fraction of .532, or over a 50% rise on the average from every base. A price move in the upward direction would be expected to carry from $1.00 per pound to over $1.53, on the average. This average puts it number 11 on the commodity uptrend ranking (see Table 2), a healthy upper-middle mover.

Coffee can move fast and far on the downside, also. Its average drop is .322, or 32.2% from the last peak. A drop from $2.00 per pound would be expected to carry prices to around $1.40, a 60-cent drop, before the average downtrend would cease, a move of almost $24,000. This large average places coffee just behind gold, the leader in downtrend sizes after financial futures with their brief history. Thus it makes an ideal candidate for trend following in both directions, up and down.

FUNDAMENTALS

Coffee has had a long and colorful part in human history. Working its way from Ethiopia through Arabic countries into Europe in the 1600s, it is a mainstay throughout the world in coffeehouses and everyday life. The New York coffee exchange was formed in the 1800s to stabilize merchant businesses after price crashes due to overabundant supplies.

A great majority (about 80%) of the coffee is produced in Central and South America. Brazil alone accounts for nearly 50% of world production, followed by Columbia with around 25%. On the consuming side, the United States drinks nearly half the world's supply.

Coffee trees require rich soil, warmth, and lots of moisture, at least 40 inches of rain per year before the berries mature, and dry weather during the harvest. Temperatures should be in the 60s or possibly a little warmer. Frosts and wind, however, are deadly enemies, as are diseases, insects, and fungi. Large wars also severely affect coffee prices. During world wars I and II, prices rose from around 10 cents per pound to between 20 and 25 cents by the end. Prices can also be affected by price agreements by cartels, as per the International Coffee Agreement of 1964. But disagreements amongst producers and the inability of Brazil to decide on and control export amounts has greatly weakened such pacts.

The trees (Aribica, the primary one) take about five years to mature, others (Robusta) take only two years. The growing period is essentially all-year round because it is grown worldwide. The crops come in irregularly. There are several crops, although a predominant amount is grown in Brazil and Columbia. Their winter (our summer) is a vulnerable period, which is watched here for freeze possibilities.

The yield, even despite the absence of freezes, is very unpredictable. A given tree can yield beans that vary in number 10 times from its minimum to its maximum, and it can produce bumper crops several years in a row followed by poor yields, for no apparent reason.

Coffee has very narrow uses. It is used as a flavoring in such things as ice cream and brandy, but its overwhelming main use is as a beverage. Its demand is very stable, for there is no adequate substitute, and it responds little to price change or purchasing power (perhaps because its cost in relation to other budget items is small and one can drink only so much).

The major determinant, then, is supply — the risk of crop ruin due to freeze and other factors, or disruptions of shipping due to wars, cartels, and the like.

IMPORTANT EVENTS TO LOOK FOR — AND THEIR EFFECTS

1. Foreign Agriculture Circular. *Coffee,* published by the USDA. Supply and weather patterns monthly or quarterly.
2. International Coffee Organization, General Statistical Documents, London, England.
3. Private all-encompassing daily newsletter by Paton in New York City.

THE RECORD: 1980–1

Parameters for the moving-average method applied to coffee are listed in Table 3, Chapter Four. The two years chosen for tests of the method were an uptrend in the 1980 contract and a volatile downtrend in 1981.

The results, using no stops at all, were erratic. Gains in 1980 amounted to over 36 cents in ten trades, while 44 cents was lost in 1981 due to sharp whipsaws against each new position. Stops of only one-half cent could have not only reduced the loss in 1981 but turned it around and produced 11 cents in net gains, while keeping most of the 1980 net gain (to around 30 cents). However, there would have been strings of losses — ten in 1981 — that could be discouraging and capital eroding. Likewise, the trader should carefully check how well his broker can execute fills — entries and exits — in this volatile market. (Refer to Chapter 5 for details on how to read Table 7.)

Table 7.

MOVING AVERAGE METHOD

CONTRACT PARAMETERS	POS	DATE IN	PRICE IN	DATE OUT	PRICE OUT	GAIN(LOSS)	MAX LOSS	OPEN DATE
COFFEE								
MAY 1980								
A P								
.100 .020								
	-1	51779	14759.00	60179	15700.00	-941.00	941.0	60179
	+1	60179	15700.00	71679	19450.00	+3750.00	0.0	60179
	-1	71679	19450.00	82079	19250.00	+200.00	600.0	72079
	+1	82079	19250.00	101179	19302.00	+52.00	750.0	82779
	-1	101179	19302.00	111279	19613.00	-311.00	311.0	111279
	+1	111279	19613.00	120479	18608.00	-1005.00	1005.0	120479
	-1	120479	18608.00	21980	17450.00	+1158.00	266.0	121979
	+1	21980	17450.00	33180	18225.00	+775.00	145.0	22080
	-1	33180	18225.00	50580	18886.00	-661.00	675.0	50580
	+1	50580	18886.00	52280	19525.00	+639.00	286.0	50680

TOTAL   +3656.00
AVE.GAIN 1095.6 AVE.LOSS   729.5

MAY 1981
  A   P
.100 .020

RATIO G/L   1.5 SUCCESS RATE 0.60 NO. TRADES 10

	POS	DATE IN	PRICE IN	DATE OUT	PRICE OUT	GAIN(LOSS)	MAX LOSS	OPEN DATE
	+1	40380	18126.00	43080	17854.00	-272.00	301.0	43080
	-1	43080	17854.00	50980	19090.00	-1236.00	1246.0	50980
	+1	50980	19090.00	61380	18565.00	-525.00	540.0	61380
	-1	61380	18565.00	62680	18700.00	-135.00	135.0	62680
	+1	62680	18700.00	70280	17381.00	-1310.00	1310.0	70280
	-1	70280	17381.00	81480	15790.00	+1591.00	244.0	71480
	+1	81480	15790.00	82180	15003.00	-787.00	787.0	82180
	-1	82180	15003.00	90880	15084.00	-81.00	81.0	90880
	+1	90880	15084.00	91180	14519.00	-565.00	565.0	91180
	-1	91180	14519.00	120380	12600.00	+1919.00	0.0	91180
	+1	120380	12600.00	121180	11800.00	-800.00	820.0	121180
	-1	121180	11800.00	122380	12700.00	-900.00	900.0	122380
	+1	122380	12700.00	12381	12708.00	+8.00	70.0	123180
	-1	12381	12708.00	31981	12637.00	+71.00	162.0	20281
	+1	31981	12637.00	41381	12170.00	-467.00	472.0	41381
	-1	41381	12170.00	42781	12870.00	-700.00	710.0	42781
	+1	42781	12870.00	43081	12648.00	-222.00	300.0	43081

TOTAL   -4420.00
AVE.GAIN   897.2 AVE.LOSS   616.0
RATIO G/L   1.4 SUCCESS RATE 0.23 NO. TRADES 17

IN THE FUTURE

Coffee is extremely volatile. It rises and falls very rapidly on supply changes — rocketing upward on freeze news, and dropping like a rock when there are good crops and Brazil fails to implement export restrictions. Coffee, now at $1.00 per pound, is very low in relation to prior trends and the great uptrend in all commodities; thus, a great bias to the upside is still in effect.

9.
Copper Profits

Copper, a vital ingredient in many industrial uses, is traded in London and New York. The U.S. exchange will be discussed here. The contract calls for 25,000 pounds, and its price is quoted in cents per pound. Trading volume has been liquid, with between 5,000–10,000 contracts passing hands each day currently. The medium is heavily used by hedgers but also has a large proportion of speculators. Each cent move in price is equivalent to $250, and each ten cents means $2,500.

THE PROFIT POTENTIAL

Copper prices have paralled the history of many commodities, especially the metals, in that price moves and trading volume were relatively small through the mid-sixties. From that point on, there have been large trends, both up and down, but quite volatile in nature. The latter half of the sixties saw prices alternately doubling and halving, due to strikes and political turmoil in producing countries and overstocking by users. (See Figure 19 for a graphical history of prices.)

The two biggest pairs of moves, however, have come in highly inflationary times: 1974 and 1980. Prices more than tripled from their respective building bases in a little over a year in each case. The bull trends, from around 45 cents to $2.45, amounted to almost $25,000 for margins starting at $1,000; very handsome returns. Moreover, these uptrends were coupled with almost as large downtrends, the result of general economy recession and a sharp drop in

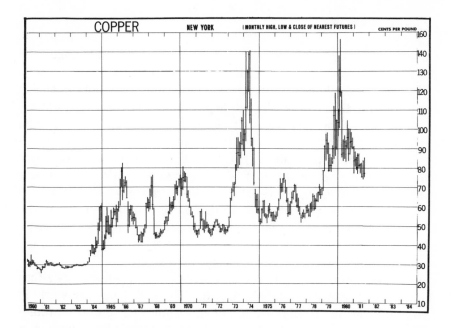

Figure 19. Monthly chart of copper prices. (Courtesy of Commodity Research Bureau, Inc., New York, N.Y.)

individual use of copper. Currently, copper prices are hovering around 85 cents, or at about the manufacturing cost of producing copper — the bare bones minimum price below which producers will go out of business in droves. The upside potential, in another bout of inflation, is great, while the downside move risk is quite small.

The red metal has a mediocre ranking in uptrend moves, placed at 16 in Table 2, Chapter 4. Its uptrend moves average size, .419, means that the average uptrend has moved from a starting price base of 100 units (say $1.00 per pound) to about 142, with margin averaging around 5 units, or 5 cents per pound. This has often been enough "room" (42 units of average move) to leave room for profits.

The downtrend average size, .252, however, is rather lackluster despite the two big downtrends in late 1974 and 1980, and accounts for its ranking of 19 in downtrend size of the 25 commodities ranked. The small downtrend potential and great volatility make copper an eratic performer (see *The Record: 1980–1*).

FUNDAMENTALS

Copper is a world commodity in both production and usage. Its price is influenced by many political and economic events.

Political and labor strife affect its production. Economic cycles in the U.S. and throughout the world influence its usage. Producers sometimes join together in cartels. Civil unrest, in Chile and Zambia, curtails production. Interest rates in the U.S. profoundly affect business use of copper and expansion. Copper companies compete amongst themselves in terms of service and salesmanship. One major method of controlling prices is to stockpile in heavy supply times so as not to be in the market and bidding up prices in lean supply times. Business cycles mean alternating increasing and dropping demand by users in expansion and contraction periods, which makes prices undulate.

Copper is produced in four major areas — South America, western Africa, North America, and the USSR. The U.S. leads the world in production at about 25%. Zambia and Chile each produce around 12%, and Russia around 14%. The major form of production is open-pit mining.

The U.S. is also the world's number one user, with industrial uses, from housing to autos to appliances and almost everything electrical (which accounts for about half of all applications) leading the way. This is why copper is so sensitive in price to general economy outlooks and changes. It has widespread use because of its high electrical and heat conductivity, corrosion resistance, strength, ductility, malleability, and its alloy properties.

There really isn't a seasonal influence on copper prices, except for a slight annual softening in summer.

IMPORTANT EVENTS TO LOOK FOR —
AND THEIR EFFECTS

1. Federal Bureau of Mines, USDA, Washington, D.C., monthly and annual data of production, stocks, and consumption in the *Mineral Industry Surveys* and *Minerals Yearbook*, respectively.
2. Bureau of Census reports on imports.
3. American Bureau of Metal Statistics reports on world production figures.

THE RECORD: 1980-1

Parameters for the moving-average method applied to copper are listed in Table 3, Chapter Four. The two years of the test consisted of a very trended year (1980) and an enormously erratic price year (1981), which were due to wildly gyrating interest rates and an up and down economy.

The results were reflective of these two years: very good in 1980 (36 cents net gain) but very poor in 1981 (76-cent loss). Unless the trader had some means of determining the oncoming wild nature of the 1981 year (through analysis of the coming national economic shape), he would have had to rely greatly on stops to protect him against enormous cumulative losses. Tight stops (½ cent) would have reduced the 1981 losses to a total of a little over a cent, but eliminated and turned into loss the fine 1980 net total gains. (See Table 8 for results details.)

Table 8.

MOVING AVERAGE METHOD

CONTRACT PARAMETERS	POS	DATE IN	PRICE IN	DATE OUT	PRICE OUT	GAIN (LOSS)	MAX LOSS	OPEN DATE
COPPER								
MAY 1980								
A P								
.100 .050								
	-1	52979	8320.00	81479	9120.00	-800.00	800.0	81479
	+1	81479	9120.00	101579	9320.00	+200.00	400.0	91879
	-1	101579	9320.00	113079	10250.00	-930.00	930.0	113079
	+1	113079	10250.00	22280	12600.00	+2350.00	750.0	120779
	-1	22280	12600.00	52380	9470.00	+3130.00	240.0	22880
	+1	52380	9470.00	52380	9470.00	+0.00	340.0	52380
TOTAL						+3950.00		
AVE. GAIN 1893.3 AVE. LOSS 576.6								
RATIO G/L 3.2 SUCCESS RATE 0.50 NO. TRADES 6								
MAY 1981								
A P								
.100 .050								
	+1	40880	10420.00	42180	9350.00	-1070.00	1070.0	42180
	-1	42180	9350.00	42580	10400.00	-1050.00	1050.0	42580
	+1	42580	10400.00	61080	9150.00	-1250.00	1250.0	61080
	-1	61080	9150.00	70380	10100.00	-950.00	950.0	70380
	+1	70380	10100.00	81580	9560.00	-540.00	540.0	81580
	-1	81580	9560.00	92280	10540.00	-980.00	980.0	92280
	+1	92280	10540.00	120480	9130.00	-1410.00	1470.0	120480
	-1	120480	9130.00	31881	8745.00	+385.00	290.0	10681
	+1	31881	8745.00	41381	8030.00	-715.00	735.0	41381
	-1	41381	8030.00	43081	8115.00	-85.00	330.0	42281
TOTAL						-7665.00		
AVE. GAIN 385.0 AVE. LOSS 894.4								
RATIO G/L 0.4 SUCCESS RATE 0.10 NO. TRADES 10								

IN THE FUTURE

Copper is an extremely volatile commodity and should be approached with the moving-average method only when super large uptrends due to massive inflation are anticipated. Because prices are severely depressed and at the margin cost of production, even a moderate inflationary period at this time could bring about at least an average uptrend move of 30–40 cents at present price levels.

10.
Corn Profits

Corn may have been invented by Indians, but modern farming grows it in a big way, making it one of the largest agricultural crops in the world. Traded principally on the Chicago Board of Trade, corn prices are quoted in cents per bushel, and anywhere from 20,000–100,000 contracts of 5,000 bushels each may change hands daily — probably the most liquid of all the commodities. Each cent move is equivalent to $50 for each contract, or $5,000 for every $1 per bushel price move. The grain is heavily used for hedging purposes with speculators a moderate influence.

THE PROFIT POTENTIAL

Corn prices have well mirrored inflation. Prior to the early seventies, prices were confined to around $1.00 per bushel, with small fluctuations. Inflation in 1974 and 1980 changed all that — costs of production and sympathy with other commodity price rises have raised corn to new price plateaus, of $2.00-$4.00, with good size uptrends and downtrends alternating. Two other major influences propelled corn prices forever past the dollar level: increased foreign demand, led by Russian grain buying beginning in 1972, and occasional drought, one in 1974 and another in 1980, which reduced yield and crop total.

Corn trends are generally slow and deliberate, with back and forth price moves about a slowly developing trendline, for both uptrends and downtrends. The first major uptrend, starting in 1972 and culminating in 1974, moved from $1.30 per bushel to $4.00, or a net move of $2.70, or $13,500. Margin or deposit requirements averaged about ten cents, or $500, so a long-term buy and hold strategy could have returned 2,600% on monies put up.

A downtrend beginning in 1974 and ending in 1977 moved about $2.00, or $10,000 per contract, with similar margin requirements during the period. A following uptrend moved the same amount, $2.00 per bushel, from 1977 to 1980. (See Figure 20 for a graphical portrayal of its price move.)

The yellow grain has only a fair ranking in uptrend average sizes for all commodities, ranking 14 of 25, with an average of .457. This means if an uptrend started at $1.00 per bushel, it would move to $1.46 before beginning a downtrend again, on average. If margin needs were 5 cents at that level (generally it is about 5% of price), there is enough room for profitable trades yielding good returns on margins.

Figure 20. Corn prices (monthly). (Courtesy of Commodity Research Bureau, Inc., New York, N.Y.)

Its downtrend average, .261, is also rather unimpressive, ranking 18 out of 25 commodities. An average downtrend, after starting at $3.00 per bushel, would fall to $2.25 or below before bottoming and starting an uptrend.

However, because of its slow, deliberate movement in the trend direction, these trend sizes, both up and down, are sufficient to make good profits, especially on relatively low margin requirements. (See *The Record: 1980–1.*)

FUNDAMENTALS

From a revenue standpoint, corn is the most valuable crop in the United States, and the U.S. usually produces more corn than the total of all other countries combined. Hence, supplies not used for our country are crucial – foreign demand plays a big part in price moves, up and down.

The crop year begins on October 1, when almost all the corn has been harvested and attention is turned toward its use and plantings for the next spring. Cash prices, reflecting both local and export buyings and farmer sellings, are the ultimate determinant of futures prices. Inventories of corn are held by farmers and the government, while demand is represented mostly by livestock feed requirements.

Three-fourths of total production occurs in the corn belt – Iowa, Illinois, Minnesota, Indiana, Nebraska, Ohio, Missouri, and South Dakota. Farmers' intentions at the beginning of the growing season, weather (drought or too much wetness, or average climatic conditions), and insects are the primary factors influencing production.

Of the production, 85% to 90% is fed to hogs, poultry, cattle, and sheep. The size of the livestock and poultry inventory is thus a basic determinant in the demand for corn. The remaining 15% is used for human consumption, or exported. Uses include seed for planting, alcohol manufacture (gasohol for cars is slowly catching on), starch for the paper, textile, laundry, and food industries, conversion into syrup and sugar for food additives, and processing into cooking oil, a base for mayonnaise and salad dressing, margarine, and high-protein concentrates. Exports are playing an increasingly important part of the demand equation, however. Eastern Europe and Asian countries, especially Russia and China, are steadily increasing their yearly imports.

Government programs influence the farmer as to how much to plant in the first place (planting intentions in the late winter) and how much to draw off and place under the government loan program. The federal government will loan the farmer, for part of his crop to set aside, a price at which it will buy the corn, thus setting a floor on general corn prices by acting as a huge buyer. The government will sell some of its stock at a high (set) price, which acts as a ceiling, because the government is, in effect, a large seller. This program, however, has not been a huge influence because government stocks have been low and the market price has greatly exceeded the "floor" loan price, so little farmer interest has been generated. Inventory stocks continue to be mainly in private hands.

IMPORTANT EVENTS TO LOOK FOR –
AND THEIR EFFECTS

1. *Grain statistical annual* (Chicago Board of Trade). Many statistics, from spot and futures price compilations, crop production, disappearance, and exports, carry-over amounts, loan rates, stocks, and so on.
2. *Feed Situation Report* (USDA). Information on crop utilization and government price-support programs, and foreign trade.
3. *Grain Market News* (USDA). Inspections for export-crop yields, production, stocks, and farms. Weekly publication, more relevant for close following of prices.
4. *Crop Production Report* (USDA). Issued around the tenth of the month, contains detailed crop estimates and production data. Most earth-shaking price changes come right after these reports.
5. *Commitments of Traders in Commodity Futures* (USDA). Monthly report showing makeup of open interest – who owns positions, large or small hedgers, larger or small speculators – and how much.

THE RECORD: 1980–1

Parameters for the moving-average method applied to corn are listed in Table 3, Chapter Four. The two years of the test consisted of a moderately undulating period of one uptrend and one downtrend in

Table 9.

MOVING AVERAGE METHOD

CONTRACT PARAMETERS		POS	DATE IN	PRICE IN	DATE OUT	PRICE OUT	GAIN(LOSS)	MAX LOSS	OPEN DATE
CORN									
MAY 1980									
A	P								
.100	.030								
		+1	60879	299.50	72479	314.75	+15.25	0.0	60879
		-1	72479	314.75	100179	313.25	+1.50	0.0	72479
		+1	100179	313.25	102679	288.50	-24.75	25.0	102679
		-1	102679	288.50	52080	271.75	+16.75	19.5	120479
		TOTAL					+8.75		
		AVE.GAIN	11.1	AVE.LOSS	24.7				
		RATIO G/L	0.4	SUCCESS RATE	0.75	NO. TRADES	4		
MAY 1981									
A	P								
.100	.030								
		+1	70280	329.50	120980	380.50	+51.00	3.5	70380
		-1	120980	380.50	43081	361.00	+19.50	12.5	10281
		TOTAL					+70.50		
		AVE.GAIN	35.2	AVE.LOSS	0.0				
		RATIO G/L	0.0	SUCCESS RATE	1.00	NO. TRADES	2		

1979–80, and two good trends in 1980–1, one up (about a dollar in length) and one down (the same length).

Gains were moderate in the first test, amounting to just under 10 cents, or $500 on about the same amount for margin. The second yearly test produced excellent profits, however, around 70 cents, or *seven* times average margin requirements. Close stops (5–10 cents) would have increased the profits slightly in the first year but dropped out a 20-cent gain in the second test. If it is possible, the trader should probably have no stops, to ensure against losing profits in the occasional and big trends around. (Refer to Table 9 for details of the two years' test.)

IN THE FUTURE

Corn is a slow-moving commodity and the trader should take advantage of possible big trends looming. Look for sudden build-up of foreign demand (especially Russia or Chinese) or poor weather. The next move should be on the upside as prices have fallen a long way and are currently near the bottom of the 1974–1980 inflation bottom.

11.
Cotton Profits

Though a pale shade of what it once was, cotton truly was "King." The fiber has been traded on futures exchanges for about a century, initially in London, then in New York and New Orleans. In the 1920s, the volume of trading reached its peak, but even as late as the 1940s the dollar volume in cotton futures equaled the trading in all other futures combined, and was several times the dollar volume of stocks traded on the New York Stock Exchange!

This discussion will center around cotton futures traded on the New York exchange. The contract, 50,000 pounds, or one bale, has considerably lessened in volume of trading since those haydays, and averages now around 5,000 contracts per day, still a good volume. Hedgers and speculators jump back and forth on both sides of the market and are equally decisive forces. A one-cent move is equal to $500; 10 cents means $5,000.

THE PROFIT POTENTIAL

Between the late 1940s and early seventies, however, cotton was about dead in volume and had little price moves, primarily because government heavily subsidized and controlled production. Since the early seventies, though, the government has pretty much gotten out of the clothing business and let cotton prices take their course. And move they have. Big moves − tripling in a little over a year, losing two-thirds of the value in one year, then tripling again − have occurred ever since.

The first move, for instance, was nearly 70 cents, or $35,000, on $1,000 margins at the beginning — an awesome potential profit for the lucky long trader.

Trends in cotton can occur steadily or sharply and can drop erratically. It can take three years to develop a long uptrend (1978– 80), but only six months to drop 30 cents, or $15,000, as it did in 1977. (See Figure 21 for an interesting price history of cotton.)

The soft white fluff ranks very high in uptrend moves (6th), with an average fraction move size of .652. This means an uptrend beginning at $1.00 a pound will move 65.2 cents on the average to $1.652 before starting a downtrend. Since margin requirements normally vary between 2 and 4 cents, the leverage potential is enormous.

Its downtrend potential is also good. With an average drop of .291 for every downtrend, it falls in just below two currencies (with few

Figure 21. Cotton—montly price chart. (Courtesy of Commodity Research Bureau, Inc., New York, N.Y.)

statistics available), ranking number 10, or just behind sugar, for commodities with a good deal of history. With prices starting at $1.00 per pound, this means the average downtrend would move to about 70 cents, a 30-cent drop, or $15,000 profit potential, before ending.

THE FUNDAMENTALS

Cotton is grown in the U.S. principally in four different regions: the South Central states (Mississippi, Arkansas, Tennessee, Louisiana, Missouri) account for about 30 percent; the Southwest, including Texas and Oklahoma, also account for 30 percent; the West (California, Arizona, New Mexico), around 20 percent; and the Southeast (the Carolinas, Georgia and Alabama), account for 15 percent of the production. The crop year begins August 1. Most is planted by May 1 and harvested in October. Supply will not only depend upon crop carry-over from previous years, but also on farmers' planting intentions and acreage allotments. Weather developments — specifically, too much moisture or too little of it — can materially affect yields and quality throughout the planting, growing, and harvesting seasons. Insects, like the famous boll weevil and bollworms, can sometimes devastate a crop. But weather (even cold, windy climates can adversely affect the sensitive plant) is the main influence on supply, and many traders carefully watch southern and southwest weather maps closely.

Demand factors move more slowly but usually have longer-lasting large effects on price. Cloth inventories, sales potential of cloth manufacturers, the quality and quantity of raw cotton inventories held by mills, domestic and foreign competition from other types of fibers and clothes, including synthetics, mill margins (some are barely profitable and their numbers are fast diminishing), and foreign inventories and prices of cotton — all importantly affect cotton demand. Traders also look at daily mill rates to determine short-term demand.

Foreign demand has significantly been picking up in recent years, including recent demand by the Chinese. Another bullish factor is the steady climb back by cotton in recapturing a lost share of the textile trade. The new clothes looks — designer jeans, jackets, shirts, and the like — are all made from cotton. Synthetics are rapidly losing their place not only because of a fad swing back to cotton, but because of the rising cost of synthetics, which are oil-based derivatives, and hence children of OPEC.

Government programs used to play a major (and at one time deathknell) role in cotton supply. At one time, 40% of the crop was under loan and 70% of the carry-over supply was in the hands of the Commodity Credit Corporation. The primary purpose of the program is to influence production by direct support payments and acreage division payments. Because of the healthy nature of the industry now, the program is quite dormant.

IMPORTANT EVENTS TO LOOK FOR – AND THEIR EFFECTS

1. *Cotton Production Report* (USDA). July through December monthly report on or about the eigth. Planted acreage, yield per harvested acre, and production by states. Price moves subsequent to release of the report can shake the earth.
2. *Cotton Situation Report.* Economic Research Service (USDA). Issued in January, March, May, July, September and October. Summarizes historical data and makes broad assessment of the cotton market.
3. *Ginning Reports* (U.S. Census Bureau). Demand analyzed semimonthly.
4. Cotton consumption and stocks at mill and in storage. U.S. Census Bureau. Twentieth of each month.
5. Raw cotton exports. Issued monthly by country of destination.
6. Various weekly figures. New York Cotton Exchange. Stocks of cotton, loan entries, and withdrawals.

THE RECORD: 1980–1

Parameters for the moving-average method applied to cotton are listed in Table 3, Chapter Four. The two years of the test were not very trended, with a 15-cent range or so one year and only 10 cents the following year. The first year (1980) resulted in a loss of 8 cents, with a gain of 9 cents in 1981. Stops would not have helped particularly.

Table 10.

MOVING AVERAGE METHOD

CONTRACT PARAMETERS	POS	DATE IN	PRICE IN	DATE OUT	PRICE OUT	GAIN(LOSS)	MAX LOSS	OPEN DATE

COTTON
MAY 1980
    A   P
 .100 .050

	POS	DATE IN	PRICE IN	DATE OUT	PRICE OUT	GAIN(LOSS)	MAX LOSS	OPEN DATE
	+1	111279	7213.00	31380	7765.00	+552.00	233.0	112779
	-1	31380	7765.00	32080	8762.00	-997.00	997.0	32080
	+1	32080	8762.00	50780	8375.00	-387.00	812.0	40980

TOTAL   -832.00
AVE.GAIN   552.0 AVE.LOSS   692.0
RATIO G/L   0.7 SUCCESS RATE 0.33 NO. TRADES   3

MAY 1981
    A   P
 .100 .050

	POS	DATE IN	PRICE IN	DATE OUT	PRICE OUT	GAIN(LOSS)
	+1	71480	8100.00	92680	8710.00	+610.00
	-1	92680	8710.00	43081	8400.00	+310.00

TOTAL   +920.00
AVE.GAIN   460.0 AVE.LOSS   0.0
RATIO G/L   0.0 SUCCESS RATE 1.00 NO. TRADES   2

Given the poor (tight) price range, the moving-average timing method fared well. (Refer to Table 10 for trading details.)

IN THE FUTURE

I anticipate much longer trends and move fruitful profits using the moving-average method in the near future. Current prices are near the past three-year low, ready for a long uptrend due to heavy foreign demand and return of inflation.

12.
Profits in the Currencies

The currency market — a fascinating market that has just recently come into its own as a vital, viable, trading medium, the futures version was started by the Chicago Mercantile Exchange in the early 1970s. Today, thousands of contracts change hands in German marks, British pounds, Swiss francs, Japanese yen, and Canadian dollars. Some other currency markets were started but have fallen by the wayside because of lack of trading interest. All sorts of interests are on both sides of the market-banks, international companies, exporters and importers, governments and speculators. Many hedgers still use forward markets and trade between themselves, in the interbank and loose international markets.

The British pounds contract consists of 25,000 pounds. The minimum price change is $.0005 per pound, or $12.50 on 25,000 pounds. Each $.100 (10-cent) change per pound for the whole contract then is 25,000 X .1 = $2,500.

Similarly, the minimum move for the Canadian dollar is $.0001 per Canadian dollar, or $10 per contract, so a $.250 price move in the Canadian dollar would be $10 X 250 = $2,500. The deutsche mark has a minimum fluctuation of $.001 per mark also, or $12.50 per contract. A $.0200 price move would then be $2,500 also. The Japanese yen has a minimum change of .00001 *cents* per yen, or $12.50 per contract. A move of $.00020 on a price graph is equivalent to $2,500 per contract. Finally, the Swiss franc has a $.0001 minimum move per franc, or $12.50 per contract, and thus a price move of $.050 on a graph would be $6,250.

(Refer to Table 1, Chapter Three for fuller details on the currency contracts: where, when, how and dollar amounts information.)

THE PROFIT POTENTIAL

Trends and good trading volume did not really get going until the late seventies, when gold, OPEC, inflation, interest rates, and the floating of all major currencies (letting them seek their own price level in the free marketplace, relative to other currencies) all propelled companies and banks to take action.

(Refer to Figures 22 through 26 for interesting pictures of various world currency moves relative to the American dollar.)

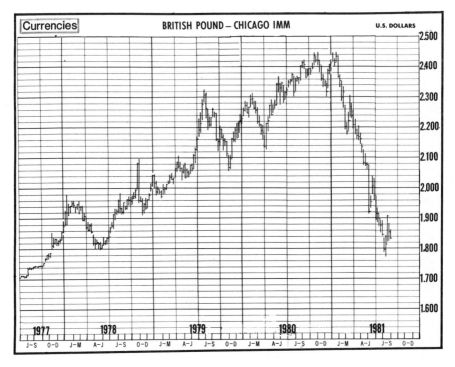

Figure 22. British pound—weekly price chart. (Courtesy of Commodity Research Bureau, Inc., New York, N.Y.)

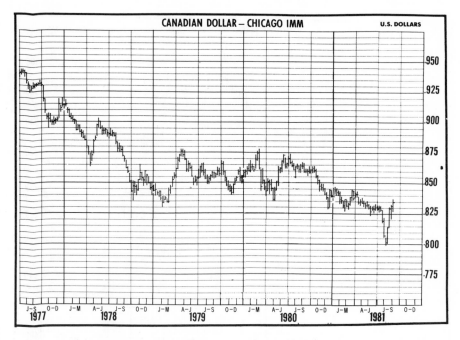

Figure 23. Canadian dollar—weekly price chart. (Courtesy of Commodity Research Bureau, Inc., New York, N.Y.)

The first impression that strikes home is that there are steady, trended periods in all the currencies. Second, there are few trends and they are long lasting. Both these factors greatly enhance the chances that trend-following methods like the moving average will perform well as money-makers.

The British pound, for instance, has had two trends, an uptrend from 1977 to mid-1980, and a downtrend since. The uptrend moved from $1.700 per pound to $2.400, a move of $.700, or 7 X $2,500 = $17,500 profit potential for long positions. The margin requirements have varied, but have averaged around $2,000 per contract. The current downtrend has dipped about the same amount, $.700, or

Figure 24. Deutsche mark—weekly price chart. (Courtesy of Commodity Research Bureau, Inc., New York, N.Y.)

about $17,500 per contract. Its uptrend ranking, 19 out of 25, is not a clear indication of its profit potential: there is only one measurement (1 trend recorded), and the profit leverage is larger than for commodities with comparable price move fractions. Likewise, its downtrend ranking of 24 is not very indicative of its profit move potential for the same reasons. As can be seen, the drop of $.700 per pound in six months could yield the trader who is short about $17,500, or more than 800% on current margins, a hearty return!

The Canadian dollar has shown only one trend — down in the past five years. It is the most sedate, little-trended of the currencies, but also the least volatile. The price move from .950 in 1977 to .800

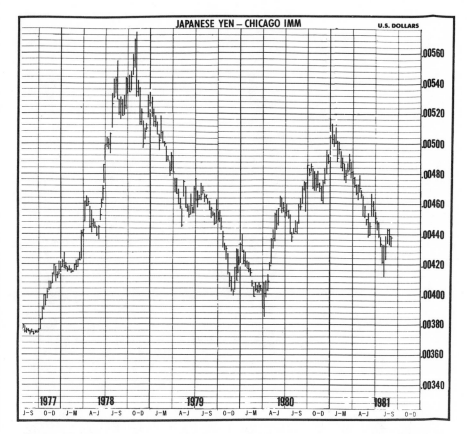

Figure 25. Japanese yen—weekly price chart. (Courtesy of Commodity Research Bureau, Inc., New York, N.Y.)

currently amount to $.1500 U.S. per Canadian dollar, or $15,000 on the contract of 100,000 Canadian dollars. Margin has averaged around $1,000, so the long downtrend profit potential has given the trader who was short 1,500 percent return on his money. This good profit potential belies its uptrend *and* downtrend ranking of dead last — 25th of 25 commodities. The ranking is not to be relied upon because of paucity of data and the fact that the profit leverage is greater here than in most commodities because of lower margins

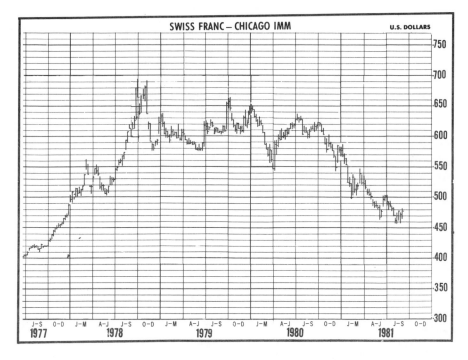

Figure 26. Swiss francs—weekly price chart. (Courtesy of Commodity Research Bureau, Inc., New York, N.Y.)

($1,000 is only about 1% of the value of the contract, around $80,000 currently).

The deutsche mark has shown two good trends — one up, one down — since 1977. Some smaller intermediary ones have also intervened. The uptrend totaled .5900 – .4200, or .1700, or over $20,000. Margins have averaged less than $2,000, so the return potential was over 1,000% — in two years! A similar downtrend of the same magnitude occurred in the next two years. Its uptrend and downtrend rankings, 17 and 9, respectively, are likewise unreliable for the same reasons given for the British pound and Canadian dollar.

The Japanese yen has shown four trends, two up, two down, that are of good size in relation to margin requirements. The first uptrend moved from .00380 dollars per year to over .00560, or almost $25,000 on average margins under $2,000 — a profit move of over

1,000% in about a year. A similar move took place on the downside the following year. Again, a great deal of profit potential that is not reflected in its uptrend (18) or downtrend (21) rankings.

The Swiss franc has had a trend move history similar to that of the deutsche mark. Its price has moved from $.400 U.S. dollars per franc to almost $.700 in late 1978, or nearly $30,000. The margin has average around $2,000, so the uptrend could have yielded a 1,500% profit for the intrepid trader who was long the franc. A similar move on the downside since then has yielded almost the same profit for the short. Its uptrend and downtrend rankings, both 8, are a little more reflective of its actual potential, but still are not accurate because of lack of data.

FUNDAMENTALS

Many things affect currency rates of conversion to U.S. dollars: international politics, wars, economic cartels (OPEC), interest rates, investment returns, balance of payments, inflation, for example. It would be exhausting to list all the possible factors influencing currency rates. Like the gross national product, currencies are reflective of broad economic issues.

Principal factors, or indicators that are closely tied to currency moves, are balance of payments, individual country interest rates, and inflation. The balance of payments is the net inflow or outflow of its total currency transactions with other countries. They include exports and imports of goods, investment by foreigners or by the country's citizens abroad, government transactions, and aids or grants. Interest-rate differentials between countries affect the flow of capital from one to the other, and the net buying and selling of one currency over the other. Inflation in a particular country, due to rising money supply, lack of production increase with production factor cost increases, or higher wages, can again affect foreign-investor capital flow.

IMPORTANT DATA TO LOOK FOR – AND THEIR EFFECTS

1. *Balance of Payments (U.S.).* Government release monthly. Higher amounts than expected shoots up the foreign currency price with respect to the dollar.

2. *Interest Rate news.*   Higher U.S. rates will draw in foreign capital, making currencies less valuable in terms of U.S. dollars.
3. *General economic news.*   New finds on the North Sea oil venture will firm the value of the British pound in relation to all other currencies, because Arabs are unloading dollars to purchase gold.   There are, of course, myriad possible items that could positively or negatively affect the dollar or other currencies.

THE RECORD: 1980–1

Parameters for the moving-average method applied to the currencies are listed in Table 3, Chapter Four.   The two years tested were generally trended for all currencies, although less so than in 1977–78.   Refer to Table 11 for trading result, for the currencies.

British pounds varied little in the 1980 contract year, between $2.10 and $2.30 generally, and then the method only broke even (lost with commissions), whereas a fairly long downtrend occurred in 1981 (a steady drop from 2.40 to 2.00), which resulted in a net profit of $.25 per pound, or over $5,000 on the contract.

Canadian dollars did not vary greatly in either of the two years, but its (small) trends moved smoothly and resulted in good gains both years.   In 1980, the net gain was almost 500 points, or $5,000, and in 1981 the gain was over 100 points, or $1,000.   The margins requirement were about $1,000, so the trader would have done very well in those two years.

The deutsche mark gave excellent profits to the moving-average practitioner, with over 500 points, or over $6,000, in 1980, and nearly 700 points, or over $8,000, in 1981.   Only $1,500 was required to trade the contract.

The Japanese yen also yielded superb profits to the trend follower.   In 1980, total gains before commissions resulted in over 500 points (over $6,000) in profits, while over 700 points (over $8,000) were accumulated in 1981.   The margin was also low, $500, so returns of nearly 400% and 500% could have been realized.

Finally, the Swiss franc also experienced good profits using the moving-average method.   In 1980 net profits amounted to over 700 points, or over $8,000 per contract, and about 20 points in 1981, or $250. Margins were $2000.

Table 11.

MOVING AVERAGE METHOD

CONTRACT PARAMETERS	POS	DATE IN	PRICE IN	DATE OUT	PRICE OUT	GAIN(LOSS)	MAX LOSS	OPEN DATE
BRITISH POUND JUNE 1980 A .100 P .003								
	+1	71779	22250.00	73179	22100.00	-150.00	250.0	73179
	-1	73179	22100.00	82779	22160.00	-60.00	150.0	80279
	+1	82779	22160.00	91279	21940.00	-220.00	220.0	91279
	-1	91279	21940.00	92679	21725.00	+215.00	0.0	91279
	+1	92679	21725.00	100579	21635.00	-90.00	125.0	100579
	-1	100579	21635.00	101079	21770.00	-135.00	145.0	101079
	+1	101079	21770.00	101579	21605.00	-165.00	180.0	101579
	-1	101579	21605.00	111579	21345.00	+260.00	0.0	101579
	+1	111579	21345.00	120779	21360.00	+15.00	60.0	112779
	-1	120779	21360.00	121179	21725.00	-365.00	380.0	121179
	+1	121179	21725.00	12880	22315.00	+590.00	35.0	121279
	-1	12880	22315.00	20180	22570.00	-255.00	275.0	20180
	+1	20180	22570.00	21980	22555.00	-15.00	80.0	21980
	-1	21980	22555.00	22180	22765.00	-210.00	230.0	22180
	+1	22180	22765.00	22280	22540.00	-225.00	250.0	22280
	-1	22280	22540.00	41080	22045.00	+495.00	240.0	22780
	+1	41080	22045.00	60380	22860.00	+815.00	160.0	41580
	-1	60380	22860.00	60480	23135.00	-275.00	345.0	60480
	+1	60480	23135.00	60980	22990.00	-145.00	150.0	60980
	-1	60980	22990.00	61080	23220.00	-230.00	340.0	61080
	+1	61080	23220.00	61680	23395.00	+175.00	0.0	61080

TOTAL   +25.00
AVE.GAIN   366.4 AVE.LOSS   181.4
RATIO G/L   2.0 SUCCESS RATE 0.33 NO. TRADES 21

JUNE 1981
A   P
.100 .003

	+1	92280	23805.00	111080	23900.00	+95.00	145.0	92680
	-1	111080	23900.00	121980	23895.00	+5.00	240.0	111380
	+1	121980	23895.00	13081	23800.00	-95.00	95.0	13081
	-1	13081	23800.00	31781	22670.00	+1130.00	160.0	20381
	+1	31781	22670.00	32681	22425.00	-245.00	140.0	32381
	-1	32681	22425.00	52981	20775.00	+1650.00	140.0	33181

TOTAL   +2540.00
AVE.GAIN   720.0 AVE.LOSS   170.0
RATIO G/L   4.2 SUCCESS RATE 0.66 NO. TRADES 6

Table 11. (Continued)

MOVING AVERAGE METHOD

CONTRACT PARAMETERS	POS	DATE IN	PRICE IN	DATE OUT	PRICE OUT	GAIN(LOSS)	MAX LOSS	OPEN DATE
CANADIAN DOLLAR								
JUNE 1980								
A P								
.100 .003								
	-1	71879	8575.00	82379	8585.00	-10.00	25.0	71979
	+1	82379	8585.00	100879	8570.00	-15.00	50.0	82979
	-1	100879	8570.00	111979	8545.00	+25.00	65.0	100979
	+1	111979	8545.00	121479	8562.00	+17.00	13.0	112379
	-1	121479	8562.00	123179	8623.00	-61.00	61.0	123179
	+1	123179	8623.00	30780	8691.00	+68.00	61.0	10380
	-1	30780	8691.00	50880	8457.00	+234.00	0.0	30780
	+1	50880	8457.00	61780	8675.00	+218.00	27.0	50980

TOTAL   +476.00
AVE.GAIN   112.4 AVE.LOSS   28.6
RATIO G/L   3.9 SUCCESS RATE 0.62 NO. TRADES   8

JUNE 1981								
A P								
.100 .003								
	-1	50580	8305.00	50880	8415.00	-110.00	110.0	50880
	+1	50880	8415.00	71580	8590.00	+175.00	0.0	50880
	-1	71580	8590.00	80680	8620.00	-30.00	50.0	71780
	+1	80680	8620.00	91680	8625.00	+5.00	30.0	81880
	-1	91680	8625.00	31381	8362.00	+263.00	40.0	92380
	+1	31381	8362.00	41381	8362.00	+0.00	7.0	31681
	-1	41381	8362.00	52981	8301.00	+61.00	18.0	41481

TOTAL   +364.00
AVE.GAIN   126.0 AVE.LOSS   46.6
RATIO G/L   2.7 SUCCESS RATE 0.57 NO. TRADES   7

Table 11. (Continued)

MOVING AVERAGE METHOD

CONTRACT PARAMETERS	POS	DATE IN	PRICE IN	DATE OUT	PRICE OUT	GAIN(LOSS)	MAX LOSS	OPEN DATE
GERMAN MARK								
JUNE 1980								
A P								
.100 .003								
	-1	60879	5385.00	61579	5475.00	-90.00	90.0	61579
	+1	61579	5475.00	80279	5640.00	+165.00	0.0	61579
	-1	80279	5640.00	81079	5700.00	-60.00	60.0	81079
	+1	81079	5700.00	100879	5800.00	+100.00	50.0	82979
	-1	100879	5800.00	101079	5860.00	-60.00	60.0	101079
	+1	101079	5860.00	101279	5808.00	-52.00	60.0	101279
	-1	101279	5808.00	110279	5810.00	-2.00	22.0	110279
	+1	110279	5810.00	111279	5754.00	-56.00	60.0	111279
	-1	111279	5754.00	111479	5826.00	-72.00	73.0	111479
	+1	111479	5826.00	120779	5846.00	+20.00	30.0	111579
	-1	120779	5846.00	121179	5943.00	-97.00	98.0	121179
	+1	121179	5943.00	11080	5946.00	+3.00	41.0	121479
	-1	11080	5946.00	41080	5439.00	+507.00	26.0	11480
	+1	41080	5439.00	61680	5662.00	+223.00	112.0	41580

TOTAL   +529.00
AVE.GAIN   169.6 AVE.LOSS   61.1
RATIO G/L   2.7 SUCCESS RATE 0.42 NO. TRADES 14

JUNE 1981								
A P								
.100 .003								
	+1	63080	5768.00	72980	5755.00	-13.00	13.0	72980
	-1	72980	5755.00	82980	5750.00	+5.00	0.0	72980
	+1	82980	5750.00	91880	5740.00	-10.00	10.0	91880
	-1	91880	5740.00	111180	5505.00	+235.00	0.0	91880
	+1	111180	5505.00	111280	5442.00	-63.00	85.0	111280
	-1	111280	5442.00	10581	5314.00	+128.00	16.0	111380
	+1	10581	5314.00	10881	5247.00	-67.00	67.0	10881
	-1	10881	5247.00	22081	4861.00	+386.00	15.0	10981
	+1	22081	4861.00	22381	4769.00	-92.00	100.0	22381
	-1	22381	4769.00	31381	4786.00	-17.00	79.0	22481
	+1	31381	4786.00	32681	4720.00	-66.00	67.0	32681
	-1	32681	4720.00	33081	4835.00	-115.00	115.0	33081
	+1	33081	4835.00	33181	4763.00	-72.00	85.0	33181
	-1	33181	4763.00	52981	4303.00	+460.00	34.0	40181

TOTAL   +699.00
AVE.GAIN   242.8 AVE.LOSS   57.2
RATIO G/L   4.2 SUCCESS RATE 0.35 NO. TRADES 14

Table 11. (Continued)

MOVING AVERAGE METHOD

CONTRACT PARAMETERS	POS	DATE IN	PRICE IN	DATE OUT	PRICE OUT	GAIN(LOSS)	MAX LOSS	OPEN DATE

JAPANESE JEN
JUNE 1980

A   P
.100   .003

	POS	DATE IN	PRICE IN	DATE OUT	PRICE OUT	GAIN(LOSS)	MAX LOSS	OPEN DATE
	-1	91179	4690.00	92079	4750.00	-60.00	60.0	92079
	+1	92079	4750.00	92479	4675.00	-75.00	75.0	92479
	-1	92479	4675.00	120679	4220.00	+455.00	25.0	100479
	+1	120679	4220.00	121479	4220.00	+0.00	0.0	120679
	-1	121479	4220.00	121779	4305.00	-85.00	100.0	121779
	+1	121779	4305.00	122879	4245.00	-60.00	65.0	122879
	-1	122879	4245.00	10280	4312.00	-67.00	75.0	10280
	+1	10280	4312.00	11580	4268.00	-44.00	52.0	11580
	-1	11580	4268.00	12380	4335.00	-67.00	77.0	12380
	+1	12380	4335.00	12480	4280.00	-55.00	65.0	12480
	-1	12480	4280.00	41080	4077.00	+203.00	7.0	13080
	+1	41080	4077.00	41580	3987.00	-90.00	100.0	41180
	-1	41580	3987.00	41680	4065.00	-78.00	100.0	41680
	+1	41680	4065.00	61680	4636.00	+571.00	45.0	42180

TOTAL   +548.00
AVE.GAIN 409.6 AVE.LOSS   61.9
RATIO G/L   6.6 SUCCESS RATE 0.21 NO. TRADES 14

JUNE 1981

A   P
.100   .003

	POS	DATE IN	PRICE IN	DATE OUT	PRICE OUT	GAIN(LOSS)	MAX LOSS	OPEN DATE
	+1	92580	4700.00	102380	4845.00	+145.00	0.0	92580
	-1	102380	4845.00	102980	4920.00	-75.00	75.0	102980
	+1	102980	4920.00	111280	4845.00	-75.00	90.0	111280
	-1	111280	4845.00	120380	4839.00	+6.00	15.0	111280
	+1	120380	4839.00	122681	5078.00	+239.00	0.0	120380
	-1	122681	5078.00	42781	4765.00	+313.00	37.0	12781
	+1	42781	4765.00	42981	4716.00	-49.00	57.0	42981
	-1	42781	4716.00	42981	4495.00	+221.00	0.0	42981

TOTAL   +725.00
AVE.GAIN 184.8 AVE.LOSS   66.3
RATIO G/L   2.7 SUCCESS RATE 0.62 NO. TRADES 8

Table 11. (Continued)

MOVING AVERAGE METHOD

CONTRACT PARAMETERS	POS	DATE IN	PRICE IN	DATE OUT	PRICE OUT	GAIN(LOSS)	MAX LOSS	OPEN DATE

SWISS FRANC
JUNE 1980
   A   P
.100 .003

	POS	DATE IN	PRICE IN	DATE OUT	PRICE OUT	GAIN(LOSS)	MAX LOSS	OPEN DATE
	+1	60479	6167.00	73079	6435.00	+268.00	17.0	61179
	-1	73079	6435.00	80979	6530.00	-95.00	95.0	80979
	+1	80979	6530.00	81379	6488.00	-42.00	58.0	81379
	-1	81379	6488.00	90679	6575.00	-87.00	92.0	90679
	+1	90679	6575.00	100879	6650.00	+75.00	30.0	91179
	-1	100879	6650.00	112979	6487.00	+163.00	88.0	101079
	+1	112979	6487.00	120779	6433.00	-54.00	67.0	120779
	-1	120779	6433.00	121179	6532.00	-99.00	127.0	121179
	+1	121179	6532.00	122079	6449.00	-83.00	127.0	121479
	-1	122079	6449.00	122179	6520.00	-71.00	71.0	122179
	+1	122179	6520.00	122879	6485.00	-35.00	40.0	122879
	-1	122879	6485.00	123179	6541.00	-56.00	60.0	123179
	+1	123179	6541.00	11580	6496.00	-45.00	56.0	11580
	-1	11580	6496.00	20680	6457.00	+39.00	49.0	11680
	+1	20680	6457.00	20880	6382.00	-75.00	100.0	20880
	-1	20880	6382.00	40980	5737.00	+645.00	45.0	21380
	+1	40980	5737.00	51980	5977.00	+240.00	34.0	41080
	-1	51980	5977.00	52180	6030.00	-53.00	73.0	52180
	+1	52180	6030.00	61680	6150.00	+120.00	19.0	52280

TOTAL   +755.00
AVE.GAIN   221.4 AVE.LOSS   66.2
RATIO G/L   3.3 SUCCESS RATE 0.36 NO. TRADES 19

JUNE 1981
   A   P
.100 .003

	POS	DATE IN	PRICE IN	DATE OUT	PRICE OUT	GAIN(LOSS)	MAX LOSS	OPEN DATE
	-1	50280	6360.00	52880	6402.00	-42.00	42.0	52880
	+1	52880	6402.00	61180	6355.00	-47.00	47.0	61180
	-1	61180	6355.00	61380	6450.00	-95.00	95.0	61380
	+1	61380	6450.00	61680	6350.00	-100.00	100.0	61680
	-1	61680	6350.00	62780	6410.00	-60.00	70.0	62780
	+1	62780	6410.00	72880	6450.00	+40.00	0.0	62780
	-1	72880	6450.00	81280	6450.00	+0.00	0.0	72880
	+1	81280	6450.00	81580	6370.00	-80.00	80.0	81580
	-1	81580	6370.00	82680	6390.00	-20.00	20.0	82680
	+1	82680	6390.00	82780	6340.00	-50.00	50.0	82780
	-1	82780	6340.00	82880	6420.00	-80.00	90.0	82880
	+1	82880	6420.00	91880	6375.00	-54.00	64.0	91880
	-1	91880	6375.00	100180	6432.00	-57.00	60.0	100180
	+1	100180	6432.00	101380	6378.00	-54.00	64.0	101380
	-1	101380	6378.00	111180	6240.00	+138.00	7.0	101480
	+1	111180	6240.00	111280	6190.00	-50.00	89.0	111280
	-1	111280	6190.00	10581	5951.00	+239.00	0.0	111280
	+1	10581	5951.00	10881	5882.00	-69.00	73.0	10881
	-1	10881	5882.00	22081	5465.00	+417.00	16.0	10981
	+1	22081	5465.00	22381	5362.00	-103.00	107.0	22381
	-1	22381	5362.00	31681	5333.00	+20.00	77.0	22481
	+1	31681	5333.00	32681	5226.00	-107.00	126.0	32681
	-1	32681	5226.00	33081	5348.00	-122.00	127.0	33081
	+1	33081	5348.00	33181	5270.00	-78.00	93.0	33181
	-1	33181	5270.00	52981	4838.00	+432.00	34.0	40181

TOTAL   +18.00
AVE.GAIN 215.8 AVE.LOSS   67.2
RATIO G/L   3.2 SUCCESS RATE 0.24 NO. TRADES 25

IN THE FUTURE

Currency futures are very trended, and tend to be for good economic reasons — balance of payments trends between countries and mostly long, slowly developing affairs, for instance.   They make excellent trading vehicles.   I expect both types of trends, up and down, to regularly alternate for long periods and good size moves.

13.
Profits in the Financial Instruments

Barely five years old, financial futures are already king of the hill in commodities. The open interest and trading volume in Treasury bonds is *twice* that of its nearest competitor, corn.

The heartbeat of the economy is interest rates, and financial futures have quickly moved into the limelight. Though initially hesitant, large institutions like banks are coming into the arena in large numbers. Trading volume is on the heels of 100,000 contracts per day, or $10 billion in value changing hands each day. Treasury bill volume has incredibly surpassed that, to the tune of nearly $50 billion!

T-bills, 90-day short-term government instruments, trade in units of 1 million dollars. Margins are around $3,000 and can move as much as $1,500 per day, a fast-paced life in these turbulent times. Treasury bonds and Ginnie Maes are in denominations of $100,000, are long-term (30 yr.) instruments quoted as a price percent of a fixed interest rate (8%), can move $2,000 per day, and have margins of $4,000. A bond may sell for 75.00, which means 75% of a bond having an interest rate of 8%, or yielding (100 ÷ 75) X 8% = 10.67%. A lower value of the bond means a higher interest rate (the bigger the discount or lower price of the bond, the higher the return or interest on the bond).

THE PROFIT POTENTIAL

Save for a short-lived rally in mid-1980, interest futures instruments have fallen in one long downtrend (which translates into a long up-trend in interest *rates* or yields on these instruments).

T-bonds, for example, have fallen from 102 to below 60, a move of 40 points over four years, or $40,000 on each contract. The margin has averaged around $3,000, so the short trader has gotten a return of 1,100% is he had held from beginning to end. Ginnie Maes (*G*overnment *M*ortgages *A*ssociation bonds representing backing of government-supported housing) have virtually paralleled T-bonds, so I will talk about bonds and mean T-bonds and Ginnie Maes.

The only rally lasted for only one quarter of a year, but meant a move of over 20 points, or $20,000, a tidy 600% return on a long position in three months if one was adept enough. (See Figures 27 through 29 for historical price graphs.)

Because of a paucity of data and the fact that a price fraction move in financial futures are much more leveraged than other commodities,

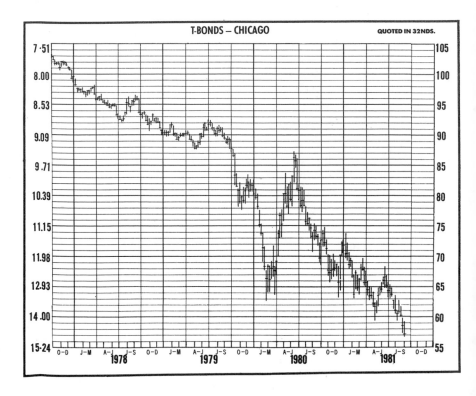

Figure 27. T-bonds—weekly price graph. (Courtesy of Commodity Research Bureau, Inc., New York, N.Y.)

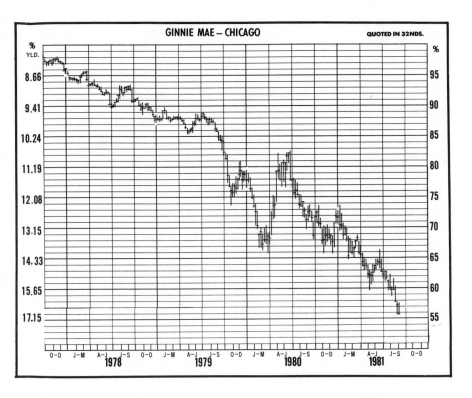

Figure 28. Ginnie Mae—weekly price graph. (Courtesy of Commodity Research Bureau, Inc., New York, N.Y.)

uptrend and downtrend price fraction rankings are inappropriate. T-bonds and Ginnie Maes normally rank last in the uptrend category, but, as pointed out above, very large profit returns could have been made in a short period, three months.

The downtrend ranking is again inaccurate for the same reasons, but T-bonds and Ginnie Maes still rank second and third, anyway.

There is no question that they are highly trended and represent real opportunity for long-term trend followers.

T-bills had two major downtrends of 10% each from 1977–1980 and mid-1980 to 1981. Each percent is equal to $2,500, so $25,000 could have been made twice, on average margins of about $2,000. This represents a return of over 1,000% on each of those moves.

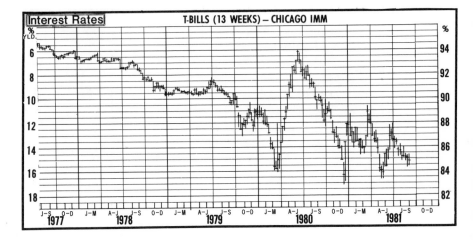

Figure 29. T-bills—weekly price graph. (Courtesy of Commodity Research Bureau, Inc., New York, N.Y.)

The sole uptrend was also 10%, over a three month period, or a profit return to the lucky long of over 1,000% in three months!

In both uptrend and downtrend rankings, T-bills have ranked exceedingly high — number one in downtrends and second in uptrends. Quite a feat!

Except for the first half of 1981 when prices were quite turbulent, price trends in all commodities have tended to be smooth.

Because of the long-term and slow-changing nature of interest-rate movements, financial futures should continue to experience long, relatively smooth trends in futures prices.

THE FUNDAMENTALS

Like currency futures, financials are influenced by many factors. Government actions, like federal spending controls, Federal Reserve credit controls, wage actions, and other economic directives can push rates either way. Company expansion plans, private bank prime-rate decisions, general public spending propensities, and even population trends (see Chapter One) can put pressure on rates. They are truly the pulse of the economy — like blood pressure, too high can mean

September 1981

Monday	Tuesday	Wednesday	Thursday	Friday
DRLDD as of 9-1-81 GNMA—CD—CBT—15 GNMA—CDR—CBT—29 Tsy Bond—CBT—29 90 Day CD—CBT—15 90 Day CD—IMM—29 90 Day CD—NYFE—14 90 Day T-Bill—IMM—24	**1** 91-182 day Bills— Announ. of Offering Construct. Expenditures— July FRB—Flow of Funds Accts. 2nd Qtr. '81 Manufacturers' Shipments Inventories/Orders— July 244/122	**2** FRB—Selected Interest Rates—August 245/121	**3** 246/120	**4** BLS—Employ. Situation— August BLS—PPI—August FRB—Consumer Install. Credit—July* FRB—Factors Affecting Re- serves of Depos. Institu- tions—Wk. Endg. 9/2 FRB—Money Supply— Week Ending 8/26 247/119
7 Labor Day Holiday— All Markets Closed 250/116	**8** 91-182 day Bills— Announ. of Offering Manufacturers' Export Sales and Orders— July Monthly Wholesale Trade—July 251/115	**9** LTD—GNMA—CD—CBT LTD—90 Day CD—CBT Monthly Selected Services Receipts—July 252/114	**10** BEA—Plant & Equipment Expenditures— 2nd Qtr. '81 253/113	**11** Advance Monthly Retail Sales—August FRB—Factors Affecting Re- serves of Depos. Institu- tions—Wk. Endg. 9/9 FRB—Money Supply— Week Ending 9/2 254/112
14 FNMA Auction LTD—90 Day CD—NYFE Manufacture and Trade: Inventories & Sales— July 257/109	**15** 91-182 day Bills— Announ. of Offering FTC—Quarterly Financial Rpt. for Mfg., Mining & Trade—2nd Qtr. '81 LDD—90 Day CD—NYFE 258/108	**16** FRB—Industrial Produc- tion—August LTD—GNMA—CDR—CBT LDD—90 Day CD—CBT 259/107	**17** BEA—Personal Income and Outlays—August BEA—Summary, US Inter- natl. Transac.—2 Q. '81 FRB—Capacity Utilization: Manufac./Matls.—Aug. Housing Starts—August HUD—Yields, FHA 30-yr. New Home Mortgages— September 1 260/106	**18** BEA—Corporate Profits— (revised)—2nd Qtr. '81 BEA—Gross Natl. Product (2nd rev.)—2nd Qtr. '81 BEA—Manufac. Capacity Utilization—June FRB—Factors Affecting Re- serves of Depos. Institu- tions—Wk. Endg. 9/16 FRB—Money Supply— Week Ending 9/9 261/105
21 LTD—GNMA—CDR—CBT LTD—Tsy Bond—CBT 264/102	**22** 91-182 day Bills— Announ. of Offering Advance Report on Dura- ble Goods, Mfg. Ship- ments and Orders— August 265/101	**23** LTD—90 day T-Bill—IMM 266/100	**24** BLS—Consumer Price Index—August BLS—Real Earnings— August Treasury Statement: (Monthly Budget)— August 267/99	**25** FRB—Factors Affecting Re- serves of Depos. Institu- tions—Wk. Endg. 9/23 FRB—Money Supply— Week Ending 9/16 LDD—90 day T-Bill—IMM 268/98
28 Export-Import Merchan- dise Trade—August FNMA Auction S&L Association Activity— August* 271/95	**29** 91-182 day Bills— Announ. of offering LTD—90 Day CD—IMM 272/94	**30** BEA—Compos. Index of Lead. Indicators—Aug. BLS—Labor Turnover in Manufacture—August BLS—Work Stops.—Aug. LDD—GNMA—CDR—CBT LDD—U.S. Tsy Bond—CBT LDD—90 Day CD—IMM Sales, Inventories of 1- Family Homes—August 273/93	OCTOBER | S	M	T	W	T	F	S
---	---	---	---	---	---	---
				1	2	3
4	5	6	7	8	9	10
11	12	13	14	15	16	17
18	19	20	21	22	23	24
25	26	27	28	29	30	31		

ABBREVIATIONS:
BEA -- Bureau of Economic Analysis   DRLDD -- Days Running to Last Delivery Day   LDD -- Last Delivery Day   HUD -- Dept. of Housing and Urban Development
BLS -- Bureau of Labor Statistics   FRB -- Federal Reserve Board   * -- Certain dates may be tentative   LTD -- Last Trading Day

Figure 30. Financial calendar. (Merrill Lynch Commodities, Inc.)

hypertension in the body (superheated rates), and a heart attack (depression) could result.

Two principal ingredients for interest rates are the money supply and government spending. The higher the money supply, the more money, and with it higher cost of borrowing, or interest-rate changes. Likewise, the more government spends, the more it must borrow, and hence represents a demand on money and upward pressure on interest rates.

IMPORTANT EVENTS – AND THEIR EFFECTS

Figure 30 is a financial calendar with many interest-rate-related events happening every other day or so. Some are more influential than others: analysts await the weekly money supply figures released each Friday at 4:10 with bated breath, and pay much attention to the consumer price index, but less so to manufacturing figures.

THE RECORD: 1980–1

Parameters for the moving-average method applied to the financial futures are listed in Table 3, Chapter Four. The two years tested were mixed in trends – 1980 saw one long downtrend and one long uptrend, also. Refer to the price graphs.

T-bonds and Ginnie Maes proved to be profitable in 1980, with net gains of 14 and 10 points, or $14,000 and $10,000 on average margins of $3,000. Ginnie Maes also proved somewhat profitable in 1981, when a gradual downtrend took place. Gains amounted to about 3 points, or $3,000. T-bonds also trended downward, but behaved erratically about the trendline, and resulted in losses of almost 14 points, or $15,000. Stops of 1¾ points would have reduced the losses to 3 points, or $3,000, but still kept 1980 gains wholly intact. Stops for Ginnie Maes of 2 points would have likewise increased gains in both years.

T-bills had two trends in 1980 and one moderate trend in 1981. Net gains were over 800 points in 1980, or $20,000 on average margins of $2,000, a return of 1,000% in one year! Gains for 1981 were smaller, around 160 points, or $4,000, a 100% return on capital (margin).

The profit results are detailed in Table 12.

Table 12.

MOVING AVERAGE METHOD

CONTRACT PARAMETERS	POS	DATE IN	PRICE IN	DATE OUT	PRICE OUT	GAIN(LOSS)	MAX LOSS	OPEN DATE
GINNIE MAE								
JUNE 1980								
A P								
.100 .030								
	−1	100879	80.37	112679	80.31	+0.06	0.0	112679
	+1	112679	80.31	12180	75.75	−4.56	4.7	12180
	−1	12180	75.75	41080	70.96	+4.78	1.0	12380
	+1	41080	70.96	61980	81.56	+10.59	0.0	41080
	TOTAL					+10.87		
	AVE.GAIN	5.1	AVE.LOSS	4.5				
	RATIO G/L	1.1	SUCCESS RATE	0.75	NO. TRADES	4		
JUNE 1981								
A P								
.100 .030								
	+1	50580	79.53	70180	76.62	−2.90	3.3	51980
	−1	70180	76.62	121980	71.12	+5.50	0.8	70780
	+1	121980	71.12	20981	67.71	−3.40	3.4	20981
	−1	20981	67.71	52981	63.71	+4.00	1.7	31881
	TOTAL					+3.18		
	AVE.GAIN	4.7	AVE.LOSS	3.1				
	RATIO G/L	1.5	SUCCESS RATE	0.50	NO. TRADES	4		

Table 12. (Continued)

MOVING AVERAGE METHOD

CONTRACT PARAMETERS	POS	DATE IN	PRICE IN	DATE OUT	PRICE OUT	GAIN(LOSS)	MAX LOSS	OPEN DATE

T BILLS
JUNE 1980

A   P
.100   .003

	POS	DATE IN	PRICE IN	DATE OUT	PRICE OUT	GAIN(LOSS)	MAX LOSS	OPEN DATE
	+1	60579	9180.00	71979	9180.00	+0.00	40.0	62579
	-1	71979	9180.00	80679	9223.00	-43.00	47.0	80679
	+1	80679	9223.00	81579	9163.00	-60.00	61.0	81579
	-1	81579	9163.00	91979	9143.00	+20.00	5.0	81679
	+1	91979	9143.00	100479	9069.00	-74.00	80.0	100479
	-1	100479	9069.00	111279	9001.00	+68.00	2.0	100579
	+1	111279	9001.00	121179	8986.00	-15.00	65.0	111479
	-1	121179	8986.00	11080	9044.00	-58.00	64.0	11080
	+1	11080	9044.00	12180	8938.00	-106.00	108.0	12180
	-1	12180	8938.00	33180	8582.00	+356.00	46.0	12380
	+1	33180	8582.00	61880	9312.00	+730.00	42.0	40180

TOTAL   +818.00
AVE.GAIN   293.5 AVE.LOSS   50.8
RATIO G/L   5.7 SUCCESS RATE 0.36 NO. TRADES 11

JUNE 1981

A   P
.100   .003

	POS	DATE IN	PRICE IN	DATE OUT	PRICE OUT	GAIN(LOSS)	MAX LOSS	OPEN DATE
	+1	50280	9128.00	51580	9082.00	-46.00	50.0	51580
	-1	51580	9082.00	52080	9149.00	-67.00	68.0	52080
	+1	52080	9149.00	62580	9166.00	+17.00	15.0	52980
	-1	62580	9166.00	71680	9190.00	-24.00	38.0	71680
	+1	71680	9190.00	72880	9122.00	-68.00	72.0	72880
	-1	72880	9122.00	100380	8897.00	+225.00	5.0	73080
	+1	100380	8897.00	102280	8866.00	-31.00	32.0	102280
	-1	102280	8866.00	121980	8747.00	+119.00	22.0	102380
	+1	121980	8747.00	10981	8769.00	+22.00	0.0	121980
	-1	10981	8769.00	12081	8826.00	-57.00	71.0	11481
	+1	12081	8826.00	12181	8766.00	-60.00	60.0	12181
	-1	12181	8766.00	12681	8841.00	-75.00	75.0	12681
	+1	12681	8841.00	20981	8761.00	-80.00	82.0	20981
	-1	20981	8761.00	30681	8782.00	-21.00	51.0	22081
	+1	30681	8782.00	40381	8783.00	+1.00	0.0	30681
	-1	40381	8783.00	52881	8504.00	+279.00	0.0	40381
	+1	52881	8504.00	52981	8539.00	+35.00	9.0	52981

TOTAL   +169.00
AVE.GAIN   99.7 AVE.LOSS   52.9
RATIO G/L   1.8 SUCCESS RATE 0.41 NO. TRADES 17

Table 12. (Continued)

MOVING AVERAGE METHOD

CONTRACT PARAMETERS	POS	DATE IN	PRICE IN	DATE OUT	PRICE OUT	GAIN(LOSS)	MAX LOSS	OPEN DATE
T BONDS								
JUNE 1980								
A P								
.100 .030								
	-1	100979	84.37	112779	83.96	+0.40	0.0	112779
	+1	112779	83.96	12180	77.34	-6.62	7.3	11880
	-1	12180	77.34	40780	71.21	+6.12	1.0	12380
	+1	40780	71.21	61980	85.78	+14.56	0.8	40880
	TOTAL					+14.46		
	AVE.GAIN		7.0 AVE.LOSS		6.6			
	RATIO G/L		1.0 SUCCESS RATE	0.75 NO.	TRADES	4		

JUNE 1981								
A P								
.100 .030								
	+1	50680	81.68	51980	77.00	-4.68	4.7	51980
	-1	51980	77.00	60680	82.25	-5.25	5.3	60680
	+1	60680	82.25	70180	79.56	-2.68	2.8	63080
	-1	70180	79.56	121980	71.00	+8.56	1.5	70380
	+1	121980	71.00	20381	68.25	-2.75	2.8	20381
	-1	20381	68.25	31781	69.62	-1.37	1.4	31781
	+1	31781	69.62	40681	63.84	-5.78	6.0	40681
	-1	40681	63.84	52981	64.75	-0.90	2.1	40881
	TOTAL					-14.87		
	AVE.GAIN		8.5 AVE.LOSS		3.3			
	RATIO G/L		2.5 SUCCESS RATE	0.12 NO.	TRADES	8		

IN THE FUTURE

Financial futures are at the core of the economy. It is locked in step to inflation. Whenever the economy gets superheated or severely depressed, interest rates will hugely trend in those directions. As I have pointed out in Chapter One, we are in for these extremes. Hence, interest rates will very much trend far and for long periods. They will be excellent vehicles for trend-following methods and will be consistently amongst the very top profit producers.

14.
Gold Profits

Gold is "young" in futures trading, having started in New York and Chicago little more than five years ago. A gala "midnight opening" started it off on the Mid American Exchange with thoughts that gold soon would be propelled upward from its price of $200. However, it seemed that American traders were "suckered" into buying it then by sophisticated Europeans, for the price plummeted immediately afterward, eventually bottoming out at $100 per ounce. Most analysts thought the gold "fad," like the hule-hoop, was over. Gold at $300 or $400 an ounce? Ha, never again!

Right now, many are saying it is cheap at $400, and a giveaway at $300 — after having dropped precipitously from a high of $850 last year. How events do change!

The principal contract calls for 100 ounces, meaning each $1 move per ounce is worth $100 on a contract, and $100 per ounce means a value change of $10,000 on the whole contract. The volume and open interest are very heavy, one of the highest of commodities, and when inflation fever, war, or crisis strike, it often is the leader in trading. All sorts of interests are on both sides of the market, industrial and corporate speculators, and institutional and governmental hedging.

THE PROFIT POTENTIAL

Figure 31, a price history graph, says it all. One big uptrend from 1977 to early 1980, a sharp, sudden downtrend in early 1980, a good size move on the upside late in 1980, and downhill ever since. The

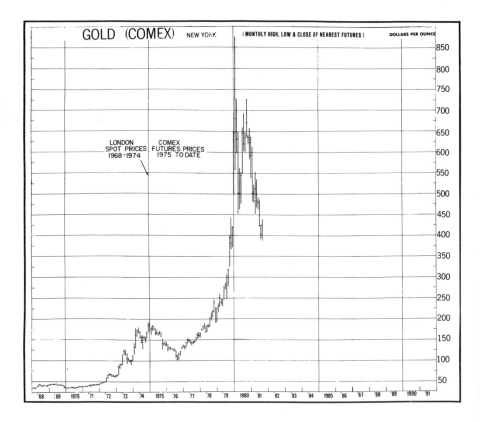

Figure 31. See monthly graphs. (Courtesy of Commodity Research Bureau, Inc., New York, N.Y.)

moves mean a lot in dollars, before even leverage (margins) is considered. The initial big uptrend moved over $700 per ounce, or $70,000 per contract. The initial margin at the beginning was as little as $1,000. This two-year move could have made a starry-eyed trader 7,000 percent profit! Even the short-lived downtrend could have returned $400 per ounce, or $40,000, on $5,000 margins (they were drastically increased), a return of 800% in three months.

Gold has been the most trended of all commodities (see Table 2, Chapter Three). It ranks number one of all commodities in uptrend moves, having an average fraction price move of 1.536. Incredibly, this means if it started on the upside at $500 per ounce, it would not halt and start a downtrend until 1268 on the average, a *huge* move!

Likewise, it ranks number one amongst all commodities, except the financial futures (which have had too few downtrends to establish a meaningful average), in downtrend moves. On the average, it falls .355 in downtrends. Starting at $1,000 per ounce, it would not bottom until it hit $644.5, plenty of room for profitable trend trading.

THE FUNDAMENTALS

Gold is mined principally in South Africa and Russia, where production is highly controlled, much like the DeBeer Corporation controls diamond production, to help keep prices high and stable. Large mining used to take place in North America (stories and histories of the western and Alaskan gold rushes still invite fantasies), but most of the veins have been played out. The yellow metal is still in short supply – legend has it that all the gold ever mined by man would stand ten feet tall on a football field.

Gold has properties much like silver and copper: brilliance, malleability, conductivity (heat and electricity), divisibility, ductility, uniformity, and, of course, small supply. For these reasons it has many uses, as currency, jewelry, and for industrial purposes. It has perhaps (along with silver) the oldest and widest usage as a storehouse for wealth. Governments, including our own until the early 1970s, used it as a backing for paper money. Because of its virtual universal acceptance as a storehouse of value, gold is highly prized in inflationary times as a haven from (paper) currencies becoming worthless due to economic havoc and breakdown in certain economies. Many Europeans have fled to gold and other commodities when their country's paper monies were devalued. Similarly, when the dollar becomes weak relative to other currencies, Arabs sell their dollars and buy gold.

Gold is also a haven for those fleeing the instability and inflation caused by local and world wars, and other crises. Mideast hostilities, the Iranian capture and hostaging of Americans, the Russian invasion of Afganistan, Polish labor troubles – all these events create concern that one or more currencies will become inflationary, causing increased purchases of gold.

It is not always clear which events will affect gold prices, nor how much or which way (up or down). Interest rates, for example, steadily climbed through 1979 and contributed greatly to gold's meteoric price rise. But after interest rates temporarily dropped in 1980 and resumed their wicked upward pace, gold started going the other way, down. Hindsight might tell us that interest rates were "breaking the back" of the U.S. economy, and gold, as a commodity along with all other commodities, was less attractive and fell in price. That is why good timing methods are needed, lest the trader do the wrong thing (buy when it is really heading downwards) and at the wrong price (too high for purchases, too low for sales).

IMPORTANT EVENTS TO LOOK FOR – AND THEIR EFFECTS

1. *Crises.* Wars, military actions, confrontations, assassinations, strikes – all create instability and lack of faith in currencies, and hence investors' flights to gold and other commodities.
2. *Balance of payments.* The heavier the imbalance toward U.S. imports, the weaker the dollar and the stronger gold. Figures are announced monthly.
3. *Buying/selling events – other commodities.* Arab selling of dollars or gold, Russian grain purchases (possibly selling gold to pay for the purchases), buying enough staple commodities to force gold upward – these and other myriad events affect gold.
4. *Interest rates, Inflation.* With moderate inflation (under 10 percent) and interest rates (under 12 percent prime rate), increases in both push gold up. Higher rates have a moderating and opposite effect on gold, as the economy is effectively dipping down.
5. *Political actions.* Embargoes of grain, selling of silver, increases or decreases in federal spending, changes in government administrations and Federal Reserve policies directly or indirectly push gold prices up or down.

THE RECORD: 1980-1

Parameters for the moving-average method applied to gold are listed in Table 3, Chapter Four. The two years tested were quite trended, with

Table 13.

MOVING AVERAGE METHOD

CONTRACT PARAMETERS	POS	DATE IN	PRICE IN	DATE OUT	PRICE OUT	GAIN(LOSS)	MAX LOSS	OPEN DATE
GOLD (N.Y.)								
JUNE 1980								
A B								
.100 .050								
	+1	82379	342.00	21980	678.50	+336.50	4.7	82479
	-1	21980	678.50	53080	545.20	+133.30	26.5	22180
	+1	53080	545.20	62580	617.00	+71.80	0.0	53080
TOTAL						+541.60		
AVE.GAIN 180.5 AVE.LOSS 0.0								
RATIO G/L 0.0 SUCCESS RATE 1.00 NO. TRADES 3								

JUNE 1981								
A B								
.100 .050								
	+1	53080	607.70	102380	684.30	+76.60	0.0	53080
	-1	102380	684.30	32081	547.40	+136.90	37.7	110580
	+1	32081	547.40	41081	496.00	-51.40	53.4	41081
	-1	41081	496.00	52981	479.40	+16.60	13.0	42281
TOTAL						+178.70		
AVE. GAIN 76.7 AVE.LOSS 51.4								
RATIO G/L 1.4 SUCCESS RATE 0.75 NO. TRADES 4								

gold rising from around $300 per ounce to $850, and back down to $450 in 1980. A smaller rise took place in late 1980 to over $700, then fell to $450 by mid-1981. (Refer to Table 13 for details on trade results.)

Net gains were $500 per ounce, or $50,000 per contract, for 1980, a return of over 3,000% on $1,500 average margins. Gains of about $200 per ounce, or $20,000 per contract, in 1981 yielded over 600% return on $3,000 margin requirements.

Two super years!

IN THE FUTURE

Because gold represents a flight from extremes, it can rocket upward in price or reflect depressionary economic tendencies by gravitating downward. In either case, there are plenty of events and influences to continually push gold either way. I foresee not only continued long, deep drops and high rises, but continual forays into new high ground as it must reflect upward in the persistent inflation to come.

15.
Hog Profits

Live hog contracts are traded on the Chicago Mercantile Exchange in 30,000 pound units. Each cent is equivalent to $300, and each five cents means $1,500. Volume of trading varies between a few thousand and ten thousand contracts per day. Trading is about equally split between hedgers and speculators.

THE PROFIT POTENTIAL

Hogs prices have been erratic, especially from 1973 on. From 1965 to 1972, prices moved somewhat sedately between 17 and 30 cents. Because feed (corn) costs changed dramatically from 1973 on, and these costs are such a higher proportion of the total cost of raising the animal, hog prices have tended to mirror and accentuate corn prices.

As can be seen from the graph (Figure 32), hog prices have really been on a roller coaster: first rising sharply from 17 to over 60 cents, back down to below 25, up again in 1975, back down in 1976, up again through 1978, down again in 1979, and currently on an up-trend from 27 to 52 cents.

The rise from 17 to 60, a net move of 43 cents, or about $13,000 on less than $1,000 margins, means a potential profit of 1,300% return on capital. Likewise, the drop to 25 cents, a net 35-cent move, or about $10,000, meant a profit potential return of 1,000% in one year.

Trends in hogs occur rather erratically, so that trend-following methods often get into whipsaw losses — first up, then down, then up rapidly.

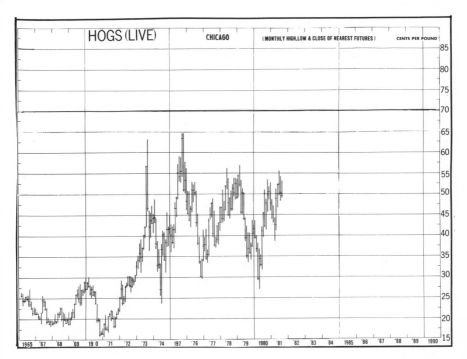

Figure 32. Hog prices—monthly chart. (Courtesy of Commodity Research Bureau, Inc., New York, N.Y.)

Because of these volatile moves, hog prices change trends quickly, and hence its trends are not long lasting and large. For that reason, hogs rank poorly in uptrends (21) with a .392 uptrend move fraction average. This means if prices start up at 40 cents, the trend may last to 56 cents before prices start downtrending. Likewise, its downtrend rank is also poor, 17th out of 25 commodities, with a downtrend average fraction size of .261. If prices were to start falling from 50 cents, the trend would end around 57 cents before moving upward again.

THE FUNDAMENTALS

The long-run supply-demand picture depends on the number of hogs raised on farms, the number slaughtered, and the amount of pork in storage. Demand is mainly a factor of consumer requirements for pork, and the supply and demand of competing products.

Iowa, Illinois, Indiana, and Missouri account for half the hogs raised in the U.S. The other six states in the corn belt produce another 25% of the hog population.

It takes 9 to 11 months to raise a pig to slaughter size, so hog expansion or contraction plans made nine months to one year ago are the central determinant in current supply. This period is one of the hog "cycles." There is also a four-year cycle, and a hog-corn ratio cycle, all of which affect the number of hogs coming to market.

Monthly estimates of production can be made by using the hog farrowing (births) of the preceding six to eight month period. Total pork production, including hams, bellies, and loins, can be estimated by multiplying the number of hogs slaughtered by the average weight. Hog production has a consistent pattern: most of the spring pig crop, constituting 55 percent of yearly production, is slaughtered in the fall.

Demand changes relatively slowly compared to production changes (essentially, the average life of the pig, 6 to 9 months). Estimates of demand starts with the quantity consumed per year per person and how this is related to its price, as well as to the prices of beef, poultry, lamb, fish, and other competitive items.

IMPORTANT EVENTS TO LOOK FOR –
AND THEIR EFFECTS

1. *Livestock and Meat Situation Reports (USDA).* Issued bimonthly, they cover general conditions affecting meats and are long-term oriented.
2. *Feed Situation Report (USDA).* Five times a year, February, April, May, August, November. General information on feed markets and hog-corn ratios.
3. *Hogs and Pigs Reports (USDA).* The most important of the reports, it is issued quarterly in the third week of the month (starting in December). Sows' furrowings, pigs per litter, total pig crop by six-month periods, number kept for breeding, number intended for market.
4. *Livestock Commercial Slaughter (USDA).* Monthly, details slaughter data by number and by weight.

THE RECORD: 1980-1

Parameters for the moving-average method applied to hogs are listed in Table 3, Chapter Four. The two years tested were a microcosm of the past eight years — some good size trends mixed in with choppy markets. Prices varied in 1980 from 34 to 41 cents, but very erratically. Nineteen eighty-one prices were more trended, moving from 46 to 57 cents. Check Table 14 for timing method trade results.

Table 14.

MOVING AVERAGE METHOD

CONTRACT PARAMETERS	POS	DATE IN	PRICE IN	DATE OUT	PRICE OUT	GAIN(LOSS)	MAX LOSS	OPEN DATE
HOGS								
JUNE 1980								
A P								
.100 .030								
	+1	60779	3990.00	71779	4140.00	+150.00	0.0	60779
	-1	71779	4140.00	81679	4175.00	-35.00	35.0	81679
	+1	81679	4175.00	92579	4167.50	-7.50	165.0	82879
	-1	92579	4167.50	110279	4250.00	-82.50	202.5	100279
	+1	110279	4250.00	120679	4225.00	-25.00	30.0	120679
	-1	120679	4225.00	121279	4552.50	-327.50	330.0	121279
	+1	121279	4552.50	121979	4257.50	-295.00	347.5	121979
	-1	121979	4257.50	10280	4547.50	-290.00	290.0	10280
	+1	10280	4547.50	10880	4247.50	-300.00	302.5	10880
	-1	10880	4247.50	60980	3475.00	+772.50	182.5	13180
	+1	60980	3475.00	62080	3975.00	+500.00	40.0	61080

TOTAL   +60.00
AVE.GAIN 474.1 AVE.LOSS   170.3
RATIO G/L   2.7 SUCCESS RATE 0.27 NO. TRADES 11

JUNE 1981								
A P								
.100 .030								
	-1	60380	4280.00	62380	4620.00	-340.00	340.0	62380
	+1	62380	4620.00	120980	5700.00	+1080.00	50.0	62580
	-1	120980	5700.00	20981	5402.50	+297.50	245.0	121980
	+1	20981	5402.50	22581	5115.00	-287.50	287.5	22581
	-1	22581	5115.00	32681	4917.50	+197.50	17.5	22681
	+1	32681	4917.50	50581	4717.50	-200.00	232.5	50581
	-1	50581	4717.50	51981	5045.00	-327.50	332.5	51981
	+1	51981	5045.00	52981	5220.00	+175.00	75.0	52081

TOTAL   +595.00
AVE.GAIN 437.5 AVE.LOSS   288.7
RATIO G/L   1.5 SUCCESS RATE 0.50 NO. TRADES 8

Net profits reflected these conditions. Barely profitable cumulatives were produced in 1980, but good profits (about 6 cents, or $1,800) occurred in 1981. This (latter) year gave a return of about 200% on capital.

Stops would have helped, bringing up net results to 11 cents for 1981, a few cents for 1980.

IN THE FUTURE

Good size trends both ways should be expected in virtually all times in the future, but, unfortunately, will alternate with choppy trends, which will probably cause frustrating whipsaw losses for this timing method.

16.
Lumber Profits

Lumber is traded on the Chicago Mercantile Exchange in units of 100,000 board feet. Prices are quoted as dollars per 1,000 board-feet. A one-dollar price move per 1,000 board-feet would be equal to 100 dollars on the entire contract. A $5 move means 500 dollars on the contract, and a $20 move per 1,000 board-feet is the same as $2,000 on the entire contract. Trading volume is relatively moderate, at around a couple of thousand contracts a day.

THE PROFIT POTENTIAL

Though making general trends (mostly upward) over the years, lumber prices have been very erratic about their growth lines. The first major uptrend, beginning in 1970, moved $100 over three years, returning $10,000 on about $1,000 average margins. The second one started in 1974, lasted through 1979, and paced off $180, or $18,000 per contract, in price move. The intervening short trend dropped about $80 per 1,000 bd-ft, or $8,000, from 1973 to 1974. The current downtrend has been more severe, dropping over $140, or 50% of its price, since 1979. (Refer to Figure 33 for a price history of lumber.)

The volatile trends produce erratic gaining and losing periods for trend-following methods.

This turbulence also accounts for lumber's relatively low standing in uptrend move ranking. Of a group of 25 commodities, it ranks only 20th, with an average uptrend move fraction of only .395. This means if prices started moving on the upside from a base of 100, the

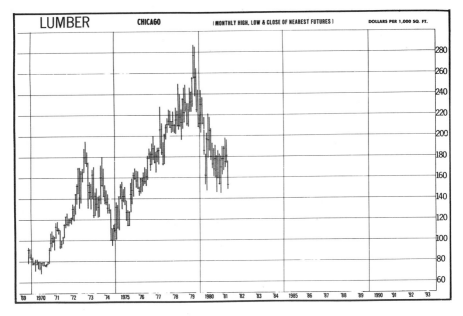

Figure 33. Lumber—monthly price graph. (Courtesy of Commodity Research Bureau, Inc., New York, N.Y.)

trend would end on the average around 140 (sometimes enough for a profitable trade, sometimes not).

The downtrends are also short-lived. Lumber ranks 23 in the list of 25, with an average drop of .234. Starting at $150 per 1,000 bd-ft, prices on average would drop to $115 before bottoming and turning upward.

THE FUNDAMENTALS

Three categories broadly affect lumber prices: demand for lumber and other wood products, total production from commercial forests, its availability, and government economic and forest management programs, from time to time.

About forty percent of softwood production (the contract's specified wood) comes from Southern pine forests, the balance mostly from western and northwestern areas.

Weather plays an important part in overall production. Three times a year hazards can develop: fire in summer, rain and snow that bog down logging operations in the winter, and precipitation that makes land areas inaccessible in the spring, reducing the length of the logging season.

The supply of certain types of lumber can vary sharply due to railroad schedule problems, for example. Substitutes for lumber, like plastic, steel, plywood, and aluminum, compete and change construction use patterns.

Demand for lumber comes from five areas: residential construction (the biggest by far), other new construction, repair and remodeling, materials handling, and other miscellaneous uses, such as furniture, manufactured products, and railroads.

The main factor affecting residential construction demand today is interest rates. Vicious, extremely high rates have torn into demand so badly currently that prices (since the price graph — Figure 33 — was constructed) have fallen mercilessly. Without a doubt, soaring interest rates can make a wasteland, a depression business out of the housing industry, and likewise for lumber.

IMPORTANT EVENTS TO LOOK FOR —
AND THEIR EFFECTS

1. *Western Lumber Facts (WWPA).* Issued monthly, it contains industry estimates of production, orders, shipments, unfilled orders, lumber inventory, average prices received, and housing start trends.
2. *Lumber Price Trends* (Inland Index, WWPA). Trend of weighted prices for inland specimens of lumber.
3. *Weekly Trade Barometer* (Southern Pine Association). Quotes and statistics on southern pine lumber production, shipments, new orders, and stocks.
4. *Housing Starts* (USDA). Monthly reports; statistics on new housing units started, total, nonfarm by ownership, type of structure, and location.
5. *Random Lengths* (Weekly lumber prices). P.O. BOX 867, Eugene, Oregon, 97401.
6. *Crow's Weekly Letter* (Weekly lumber prices). C. C. Crow Publications, Inc., Terminal Sale Building, Portland, Oregon, 97205.

THE RECORD: 1980–1

Parameters for the moving-average method applied to lumber are listed in Table 3, Chapter Four. The two years tested were a mixture of a few good downtrends mixed in with undulating, choppy markets very much representative of the types of markets in lumber over the life of its history.

In 1980, prices bounced back and forth, then dropped $80 to $150. The moving-average method did poorly at first, then recouped at the end, and ended up with a small net gain of $5, or $500, on average margins of around $1,000. A downtrend also occurred in 1981, and this time the method captured most of the move for a net gain of about $40, or $4,000, for a return of nearly 400%. (See trading details in Table 15.)

Table 15.

MOVING AVERAGE METHOD

CONTRACT PARAMETERS	POS	DATE IN	PRICE IN	DATE OUT	PRICE OUT	GAIN(LOSS)	MAX LOSS	OPEN DATE
LUMBER								
MAY 1980								
A P								
.100 .050								
	+1	91079	234.00	101679	215.80	−18.20	19.8	101679
	−1	101679	215.80	12180	236.20	−20.40	20.4	12180
	+1	12180	236.20	22980	216.30	−19.90	21.2	22980
	−1	22980	216.30	51580	152.20	+64.10	3.0	30580
	TOTAL					+5.60		
	AVE.GAIN	64.1	AVE.LOSS	19.5				
	RATIO G/L	3.2	SUCCESS RATE	0.25	NO. TRADES	4		

CONTRACT PARAMETERS	POS	DATE IN	PRICE IN	DATE OUT	PRICE OUT	GAIN(LOSS)	MAX LOSS	OPEN DATE
MAY 1981								
A P								
.100 .050								
	+1	41480	183.50	82580	205.00	+21.50	3.9	41580
	−1	82580	205.00	42381	183.80	+21.20	15.0	112180
	+1	42381	183.80	43081	178.40	−5.40	5.8	43081
	TOTAL					+37.30		
	AVE.GAIN	21.3	AVE.LOSS	5.4				
	RATIO G/L	3.9	SUCCESS RATE	0.66	NO. TRADES	3		

IN THE FUTURE

The severe interest rate crunch and inflation should continue to pound lumber prices down even further, to very low prices (around $70 per 1,000 bd-ft perhaps). At that point, a general economic recovery and explosive lumber price rise should begin. One extreme tends to begat the other: a sharp rise brings about a counterwaiting sharp drop, and vice versa.

17.
Orange Juice Profits

Frozen concentrated orange juice is traded on the New York Cotton Exchange in units of 15,000 pounds per contract. Prices are quoted in cents per pound, which means a 1-cent move per pound in price is equivalent to $150 for the contract. Similarly, a 10-cent move means a $1,500 change in the value of the contract. Trading volume has varied, depending upon the year and time of season, and has ranged from under a thousand to over ten thousand contracts per day. Although there are a number of hedgers in the market, it is a favorite of speculators who watch the winter weather as it progresses south.

THE PROFIT POTENTIAL

Orange juice has made major trends in both directions, but by far the largest moves have occurred in uptrends. Many speculators "gear up" and buy contracts before or at the inception of winter in the U.S., anticipating a freeze in Florida and damage to the orange crop, with concommitant sudden rises in price. Such freezes have occurred on four occasions in the past. (See Figure 34 for a dramatic portrayal of orange juice price moves.)

In 1968, prices shot up to over 60 cents a pound from around 30 cents, due to cold weather. The net price change, 30 cents, amounted to $4,500 on margins of under $1,000, about a 500% return on "cold weather" capital.

A similar event happened in 1971, but the largest rise to date occurred in 1977, when frost not only damaged the fruit but the

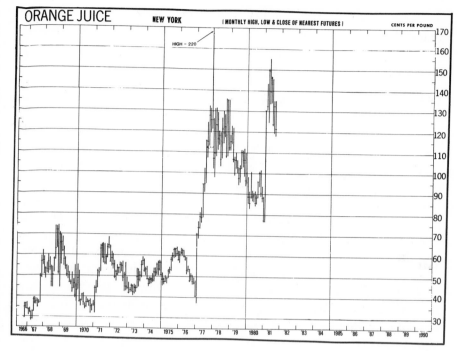

Figure 34. (Courtesy of Commodity Research Bureau, Inc., New York, N.Y.)

trees themselves, and prices shot up to $2.20 from around $.40, a gigantic move of $1.80, or $27,000 on margins of about $1,000, a 27-fold return in less than a year! In all fairness, a subsequent hurricane in the fall damaged the trees, to extend the price move.

Another big move happened in 1981, when prices rose almost 80 cents, or $12,000, from its starting point, as about 25% of the crop was ruined by a January cold snap.

Orange juice has an excellent ranking in uptrend average moves. Ranking number 5, it has an average uptrend fraction move of .673. If prices started in an uptrend from $1.00 per pound, the uptrend would continue on the average to $1.67 before stopping and starting a downtrend.

Its downtrend ranking is only mediocre, at 13 in a field of 25. The average downtrend fraction is .283. If a downtrend were to begin at $1.00, it would fall on the average to $.72 before turning and proceeding in an uptrend.

THE FUNDAMENTALS

Florida produces about one-fourth of the entire world's supply of oranges. Three-quarters of the produce ends up as frozen concentrate.

Demand for frozen orange juice not only depends on population size and purchasing power, but also on industry promotional efforts (like special discounts at the supermarket). Demand is thought to be more elastic than that for other commodities.

However, supply is the main determinant of prices. The amount in storage, the size of the crop produced, the movement to retail, the number of trees, the number of fruits per tree, the size of the oranges, and the drop rate all affect the supply available for concentrate sales.

The principal, and perhaps only, factor in crop production, though, is weather. Freezes, hurricanes, droughts, or too much rain can propel prices upward as significant chunks of current crop are destroyed, sometimes along with the trees themselves. Sudden heat waves and insects can create havoc, too.

IMPORTANT EVENTS TO LOOK FOR –
AND THEIR EFFECTS

1. *Fruit Situation Report* (USDA). Four times a year available supply and consumption figures are released.
2. *Summary of Citrus Fruit Industry* (USDA). October release or orange crop estimate for approaching season.
3. *Crop Production Reports* (USDA). Six times a year summary of conditions of many citrus crops, and comparisons with the prior year.
4. *Monthly Cold Storage Reports* (USDA). Released mid-month, the report indicates frozen orange juice stocks.

THE RECORD: 1980-1

Parameters for the moving-average method applied to frozen concentrated orange juice are listed in Table 3, Chapter Four. The two years covered included a big uptrend in 1981, and dormant markets in 1980.

Choppy price moves in 1980 produced no gain (but virtually no loss either) for the timing method.   In 1981, however, a big move from 90 cents to $1.40 per pound gave the moving-average method a nifty net gain of almost 55 cents, or over $16,000 for a margin around $1,000.   Tight stops may have increased profits even more for both years. (Refer to Table 16 for trading details.)

Table 16

MOVING AVERAGE METHOD

CONTRACT PARAMETERS	POS	DATE IN	PRICE IN	DATE OUT	PRICE OUT	GAIN(LOSS)	MAX LOSS	OPEN DATE
FCOJ								
MAY 1980								
A P								
.100 .020								
	+1	51779	10150.00	61179	9760.00	−390.00	480.0	61179
	−1	61179	9760.00	70679	9825.00	−65.00	65.0	70679
	+1	70679	9825.00	90779	10200.00	+375.00	0.0	70679
	−1	90779	10200.00	92179	10780.00	−580.00	600.0	92179
	+1	92179	10780.00	101579	10300.00	−480.00	480.0	101579
	−1	101579	10300.00	121379	10190.00	+110.00	0.0	101579
	+1	121379	10190.00	123179	9790.00	−400.00	440.0	123179
	−1	123179	9790.00	30380	9115.00	+675.00	210.0	10480
	+1	30380	9115.00	32480	9300.00	+185.00	0.0	30380
	−1	32480	9300.00	51680	8755.00	+545.00	160.0	32780

TOTAL   −25.00
AVE.GAIN 378.0 AVE.LOSS   383.0
RATIO G/L   0.9 SUCCESS RATE 0.50 NO. TRADES 10

MAY 1981								
A P								
.100 .020								
	+1	40980	9455.00	60980	9170.00	−285.00	285.0	60980
	−1	60980	9170.00	71580	9455.00	−285.00	285.0	71580
	+1	71580	9455.00	101380	9945.00	+490.00	210.0	72580
	−1	101380	9945.00	11281	8970.00	+975.00	0.0	101380
	+1	11281	8970.00	31381	13670.00	+4700.00	0.0	11281
	−1	31381	13670.00	32581	13970.00	−300.00	300.0	32581
	+1	32581	13970.00	41381	14065.00	+95.00	0.0	32581
	−1	41381	14065.00	43081	13960.00	+105.00	275.0	42831

TOTAL   +5495.00
AVE.GAIN 1273.0 AVE.LOSS   290.0
RATIO G/L   4.3 SUCCESS RATE 0.62 NO. TRADES   8

IN THE FUTURE

While not regularly every year, orange juice has experienced some sort of bad weather phenomenon almost every other year, and consequently big uptrends thereafter.

I do not expect bad weather to repeat like clockwork every year or even every other year, but I do anticipate many continued weather ramifications in the future.   The odds strongly favor many more supertrends in the offing.

18.
Pork Belly Profits

Frozen pork bellies are traded on the Chicago Mercantile Exchange in units of 38,000 pounds per contract. Prices are quoted in cents per pound, which means a one-cent price move is equal to $380 on the contract. A 10-cent move means a $3,800 change on the entire contract.

Pork bellies were once the prima donna of futures trading, especially for speculators, in the early years of its life. Trading volume was well over 10,000 contracts, closer to 20,000, and led all markets in that category. Violent price changes in the middle seventies sharply reduced the volume of trading, however, and today it is a pale shadow of what it used to be.

Bellies continue to have the greatest speculators to hedgers ratio of all commodities.

THE PROFIT POTENTIAL

Pork bellies have a history of many long trends and also many whipsaw periods. Figure 35 aptly depicts those broad up and down price movements.

The very first price move, in 1965, brought prices from 20 cents to about 55 cents, or 35 cents in one year. This amounted to over $13,000 on margins of about $1,000, a return of 1,300% in a short time. Similar moves have occurred since then — at least five moves of that size (35 cents) or *larger* on the upside. One, beginning in 1974 and ending a year later, went up a total of 75 cents, or over $28,000.

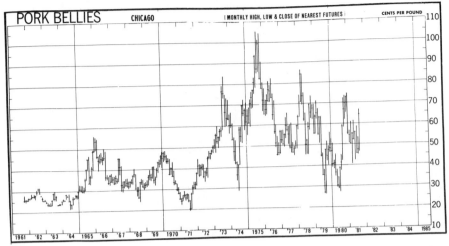

Figure 35. Pork bellies—monthly graph. (Courtesy of Commodity Research Bureau, Inc., New York, N.Y.)

Downtrends have also yielded great profit opportunities. In 1970, prices dropped from about 50 cents to 20 cents, again in a year's time, for a total move of 30 cents, or about $11,000, for over a 1,000% return on capital on the short side.

Larger downtrends have occurred since then. In 1973, a drop of about 55 cents from 85 cents occurred in less than one year, for a profit potential for short sales of over $20,000.

At least four other big drops have occurred thereafter.

The trader has plenty of profit-making opportunity in pork bellies.

Because of many periods of price turbulence, however, bellies rank only in the middle of commodities (13th) with respect to uptrend potential, with an average uptrend fraction move size of .464. This means an uptrend starting at 50 cents on the average will move to 73.20 before topping out.

Likewise, its downtrend ranking, 12th of 25 commodities, is only average for the same reasons (many intervening choppy markets). Its downtrend average of .290 means that a downtrend starting at 70 cents will fall to about 50 cents, or a 20-cent fall, before bottoming out and proceeding in an uptrend.

Because of the sharply turning and choppy markets, the trader must have good, quickly turning timing methods.

THE FUNDAMENTALS

Pork bellies are uncured bacon that come from the underside of a hog.

The production of pork bellies is solely dependent upon the size of the pig crop. Refer to the chapter on hogs to understand the determinants of pig crop sizes.

Storage stocks of bacon are determined by previous hog slaughter and consumption of hogs and bacon. Slaughter usually exceeds demand from November until April or May, in which time cold storage of bacon tends to build up and put pressure on pork belly prices.

Forecasting total pork belly supplies means adding the weight of cold storage supplies to that from the number of hogs available for slaughter (and hence near to future bacon slicings).

Prices behave sensitively to changes in cold storage stocks or bacon inventory, because in most years consumption and supply of new bacon (from hog slaughter) are nearly equal, and the inventory level is the "excess" supply that governs which way prices will go: continued large inventories will suppress prices, while large outflows of bacon and low inventories will make prices skyrocket. Storage stocks become most important late in the contract year (May and June) when consumption exceeds production.

An additional sensitivity factor in the market is the perishability of bellies. They cannot last more than eight months in storage, which tends to add to seasonal price fluctuation. By October, carry-over stocks in storage remain very small — less than one week's consumption. Because of the hog slaughter schedule and the inventory use pattern, belly prices tend to be lowest in the fall and winter and peak (with low inventory and no slaughter yet) between July and September.

Consumption, or demand, changes little. It is fairly constant, except at very low (25–30 cents) or very high (over $1.00) prices.

IMPORTANT EVENTS TO LOOK FOR —
AND THEIR EFFECTS

1. *Livestock and Meat Situation Reports* (USDA). Bimonthly report on general conditions affecting meat markets.

2. *Feed Situation Reports* (USDA). Published five times a year, in February, April, May, August, and November. Hog-corn ratios.
3. *Hogs and Pigs Report* (USDA). Released quarterly, in the third week, it contains total pig-crop, number kept for breeding, number intended for market.
4. *Cold Storage Reports* (USDA).   Monthly all-important release (in mid-month) on holdings as of the 1st of the month.

THE RECORD: 1980–1

Parameters for the moving-average method applied to pork bellies are listed in Table 3, Chapter Four.   The two years covered two moderately trended years — one in 1980, when prices varied from 31 to 50 cents, and the other in 1981, in which prices went generally from 50 to 70 cents.

Despite sharp turns and choppy markets, the method performed well in both years.   About 15 cents, or almost $6,000 per contract, was made in each year, or about 400% return on $1,500 margins or capital requirements.   Stops of 1 cent or more would have helped in 1981, increasing profits by about 5 cents.   No change would have been registered in 1980 profits, however.   Details of the trades can be found in Table 17.

IN THE FUTURE

The very nature of pork bellies — the hog slaughter time, cold storage inventories, and perishability — portends much of the same, big trends with turbulent periods in between, in the future.   Trend-following methods can and will do well, but will be subject to whip-saws and hence must be adaptable and sensitive.

Table 17.

MOVING AVERAGE METHOD

CONTRACT PARAMETERS	POS	DATE IN	PRICE IN	DATE OUT	PRICE OUT	GAIN(LOSS)	MAX LOSS	OPEN DATE
PORK BELLIES								
MAY 1980								
A P								
.100 .050								
	−1	50479	5195.00	82079	4510.00	+685.00	65.0	52379
	+1	82079	4510.00	92579	4515.00	+5.00	325.0	82879
	−1	92579	4515.00	102379	4780.00	−265.00	360.0	100279
	+1	102379	4780.00	120479	4952.50	+172.50	200.0	102479
	−1	120479	4952.50	31880	4570.00	+382.50	507.5	121779
	+1	31880	4570.00	32480	4125.00	−445.00	445.0	32480
	−1	32480	4125.00	52280	3160.00	+965.00	0.0	32480

TOTAL   +1500.00
AVE.GAIN   442.0 AVE.LOSS   355.0
RATIO G/L   1.2 SUCCESS RATE 0.71 NO. TRADES   7

MAY 1981								
A P								
.100 .050								
	−1	41780	4655.00	61180	4785.00	−130.00	320.0	50680
	+1	61180	4785.00	100380	6415.00	+1630.00	95.0	61780
	−1	100380	6415.00	101080	7117.50	−702.50	765.0	101080
	+1	101080	7117.50	120880	6857.50	−260.00	347.5	111280
	−1	120880	6857.50	21081	6027.50	+830.00	0.0	120880
	+1	21081	6027.50	22581	5572.50	−455.00	455.0	22581
	−1	22581	5572.50	32681	5112.50	+460.00	27.5	22681
	+1	32681	5112.50	43081	5215.00	+102.50	0.0	32681
	−1	43081	5215.00	43081	5215.00	+0.00	0.0	43081

TOTAL   +1475.00
AVE.GAIN   755.6 AVE.LOSS   309.5
RATIO G/L   2.4 SUCCESS RATE 0.44 NO. TRADES   9

19.
Silver Profits

Silver is traded on various exchanges in the world, but the New York Commodity Exchange is by far the volume leader after years of rivalry with the Chicago Board of Trade.

The contract calls for 5,000 ounces presently (there is pressure to reduce the size to 1,000 ounces), and is quoted in dollars per ounce. A $1.00 change per ounce of silver means $5,000 on the contract, and a $4.00 change means a $20,000 huge increase in its value. Trading volume was small at first, when prices were around $1.30, the government-supported price. Volume increased tremendously to 50,000 contracts a day until in 1980 it became the commodity volume leader. However, a huge bust in price sharply diminished volume to the present five thousand contracts.

Silver has a great proportion of its trading in the hands of speculators, second only to pork bellies.

THE PROFIT POTENTIAL

Like a volcano exploding, silver gave traders a taste of what was to come in 1974, when it soared from $1.50 to almost $5.00 per ounce. The anticipation of government sale of silver stocks had steadily pushed it up. Since the margin at the time was only 20 cents, the return on capital for those holding long contracts was almost 2,000%.

For a long period, though, from 1974 to 1979, prices went essentially sideways and resulted in losses to trend followers.

The thundering roar came in 1979. Due to a number of factors — increasing inflation, depletion of government silver stocks, and large buying by the Hunts of Texas – the ground shook and prices catapulted from around $5 to over $50 per ounce in less than one year. The profit, had one been perceptive enough, amounted to $45 per ounce at the height, a return of 220-fold on initial margins, or 22,000%!

Downtrends have given the trader ample opportunity for profit also. The collapse following the meteoric 1979 rise went initially to around $10 from $50 in less time than it took to rise to $50 for almost the same profit (not the same return – margins had risen dramatically). A second downtrend, after a momentary recovery of prices, dropped prices from $25 to $10 per ounce, and prices have been pushing downward since. Figure 36 depicts the price saga for silver.

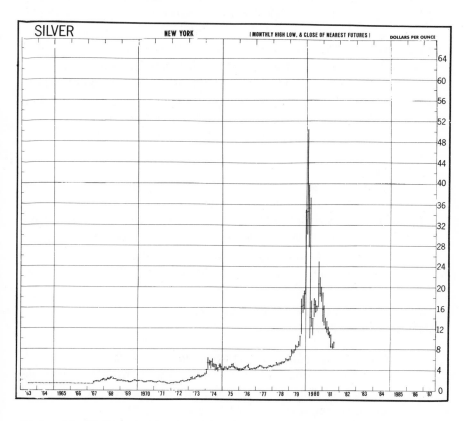

Figure 36. Silver—monthly chart. (Courtesy of Commodity Research Bureau, Inc., New York, N.Y.)

Silver ranks very high, 3rd, in the uptrend move size averages of the 25 commodities, with a 1.188 figure. An uptrend beginning at $10 per ounce could be expected to rise to $21.90 before topping out and starting a downtrend.

It does not rank too high in downtrends, however. It places 16th amongst 25, with an average of .262. This means if prices started from $20 per ounce, the prices would fall until bottoming at $14.75.

THE FUNDAMENTALS

Silver's main uses have been for coinage and as stock for currency backing for the United States. The U.S. government had been buying and stockpiling since 1934 for these purposes, and so its policy (of selling at $1.30 per ounce to maintain the price) had kept the price fixed and low over the years. In 1967, the Treasury halted sales and the market has been free to seek its level ever since.

Prior to World War II, production comfortably exceeded consumption by a good margin. However, industrial usage has climbed dramatically and most of the bigger mines have been depleted, leaving mostly production of silver as an offshoot of copper, zinc, lead, and tin mining.

Most of the world's silver is produced by the U.S., Peru, Mexico, Canada, and the USSR. Labor strikes in Chile and Peru can cause disruptions in copper and silver production and affect prices.

Inflation and hoarding binges are the strongest influences, however. People flee from currencies to hard currencies like silver in times of crises, war, and high inflation. Likewise, hoarding occurs if speculators fear cutbacks in production and large increases in usage.

IMPORTANT EVENTS TO LOOK FOR –
AND THEIR EFFECTS

1. *War, crises, calamities, strikes, and confrontations.* Violent, strife-laden situations cause investors to forsake currencies because of fear of instability, and consequential buying of precious metals takes place.
2. *Government economic policy changes.* Federal Reserve money policy, silver sales, budget revisions, and more, affect the demand and supply for silver.

THE RECORD: 1980-1

Parameters for the moving-average method applied to silver are listed in Table 3, Chapter Four. The past two years were replete with soaring and massively dropping trends. It was a good environment for trend-following methods. Prices rose from $9 per ounce to over $40, then dropped to $12 in 1980. Up and down action characterized 1981 prices, when silver quotes vascillated between $11 and $21 per ounce several times.

The timing method did very well in both years. In 1980, net gains amounted to over $40 per ounce, or $200,000 on margins that ranged from $1,000 to $20,000. Whichever figure is used, the profit return on capital was tremendous, nothing short of spectacular. Though the price ranges were tighter in 1981, big profits of over $18, or $90,000, were accumulated. (Refer to Table 18 for details on the exciting trades.)

Table 18.

MOVING AVERAGE METHOD

CONTRACT PARAMETERS	POS	DATE IN	PRICE IN	DATE OUT	PRICE OUT	GAIN(LOSS)	MAX LOSS	OPEN DATE
SILVER(N.Y.)								
MAY 1980								
A P								
.100 .050								
	+1	50779	908.70	20480	3425.00	+2516.30	23.2	50979
	-1	20480	3425.00	20880	3825.00	-400.00	400.0	20880
	+1	20880	3825.00	22080	3485.00	-340.00	340.0	22080
	-1	22080	3485.00	52380	1196.00	+2289.00	275.0	30580
		TOTAL				+4065.30		
		AVE.GAIN 2402.6 AVE.LOSS 370.0						
		RATIO G/L 6.4 SUCCESS RATE 0.50 NO. TRADES 4						

MAY 1981								
A P								
.100 .050								
	-1	40380	1962.00	53080	1514.00	+448.00	38.0	40980
	+1	53080	1514.00	102080	2122.00	+608.00	0.0	53080
	-1	102080	2122.00	31881	1330.00	+792.00	48.0	102280
	+1	31881	1330.00	33181	1203.00	-127.00	160.0	33181
	-1	33181	1203.00	43081	1100.00	+94.00	45.0	40681
		TOTAL				+1815.00		
		AVE.GAIN 485.5 AVE.LOSS 127.0						
		RATIO G/L 3.8 SUCCESS RATE 0.80 NO. TRADES 5						

IN THE FUTURE

Silver is a very explosive commodity. It mirrors instability, increasing demand, and shrinking production, and is a pretty sure winner on the upside many times in the future. I expect similar big trends in the near future, though not quite as dramatic as the 1980 price bulge.

Trend-following methods must have this in their portfolios.

20.
Profits in the Soybean Complex

The soybean complex is traded on the Chicago Board of Trade. Soybeans are traded in units of 5,000 bushels, and quoted in cents per bushel. A one-cent change is equal to $50, and a $1 price change means $5,000 on the contract. Soybean oil trades in units of 60,000 pounds, and its price is quoted in cents per pound. A one-cent move per pound means $600 on the contract, and 5 cents in equivalent to $3,000. Soybean meal trades in units of 100 tons per each contract, and is quoted in dollars per ton. A $1 move means $100 on the contract, while a $40 price change is equivalent to $4,000 on the entire contract.

Trading volume has been large for the soybean complex. Soybeans rank third behind bonds and corn in current volume standing, and typically trade 20,000 to 30,000 contracts a day. Soybean meal trades well also, averaging in the 10,000 contracts a day neighborhood, and soybean oil is just behind meal at slightly less than 10,000 contracts per day.

The trading is well spread out amongst large and small hedging interests, and speculators. The latter tend to trade soybeans for its longer price moves and greater leverage at times.

THE PROFIT POTENTIAL

The soybean complex has been a favorite over the years of speculators seeking long trends. Although a relatively dormant price period prevailed during the 1950s and 1960s, volatile price movements have occurred in the seventies. At least four major uptrends and three large downtrends have given the trader profit opportunities in the past ten years. Refer to Figures 37, 38, and 39 for price graphs on soybeans, soybean meal, and soybean oil.

Soybeans rose in 1973 from just over $3 per bushel to almost $13, an incredible move of $10, or $50,000. Margins at the beginning were around 20 cents per bushel, or $1,000, so the profit return on this gigantic uptrend for the lucky holder would have amounted to 5,000%, surpassed only by silver's equally huge move in 1979. On the short side, a downtrend starting in 1973 dropped prices from the $13 area to less than $6, or about a $7 move. This could have given the short trader a profit of $35,000, with higher margin requirements.

Soybeans rank 10th in uptrend move fraction average out of 25 commodities, with an average uptrend of .526, or 52.6 percent. This means that if prices started at $7.00 per bushel, the move on the upside would continue on the average to about $10.70 before topping

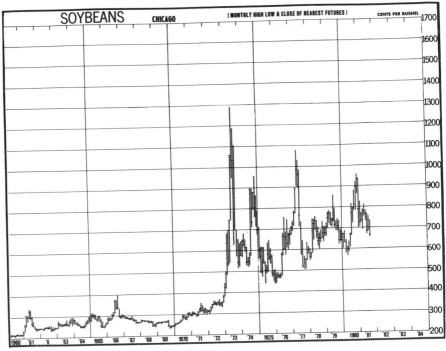

Figure 37. Soybean monthly price chart. (Courtesy of Commodity Research Bureau, Inc., New York, N.Y.)

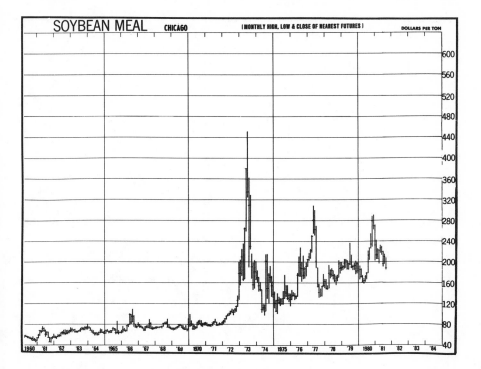

Figure 38. Soybean meal price chart. (Courtesy of Commodity Research Bureau, Inc., New York, N.Y.)

out and starting a downtrend.   Likewise, it ranks almost the same in downtrend average sizes, 11th, out of 25 commodities. Its average of .291 means that if prices started falling from $10.00 per bushel, the downtrend would bottom on the average at about $7.10 before starting on the upside.

Soybean meal prices have pretty much mirrored that of soybeans. In 1973 prices also rose quite a bit — from about $100 per ton to over $440, a difference of $340 per ton, or $34,000 on each contract. Margin (capital) requirements were less than $1,000 at first, so a 3,400% return on capital for a lucky long trader was not unheard of. A subsequent downtrend dropped prices from the $440 level to the same starting price, and could have yielded the short trader an equivalent $34,000 on capital. Several other sizable uptrends and downtrends (but not as large) have occurred since then.

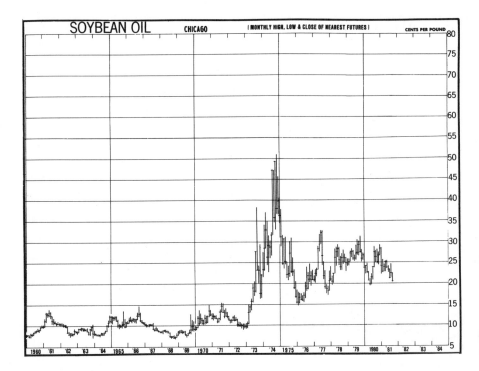

Figure 39. Soybean oil price chart. (Courtesy of Commodity Research Bureau, Inc., New York, N.Y.)

Soybean meal's uptrend ranking is 9, just ahead of soybeans, with an average of .593. This translates into prices moving on the average from $200 to $320 before a downtrend sets in. Its rank in downtrends is even higher – 6 – because of an average drop of .333, or 33.3%. A downtrend starting at $300 would fall to $200 before bottoming and starting an uptrend.

Soybean oil prices again are similar to that for soybeans and soybean meal. In the same year of 1973 prices started at 10 cents per pound and eventually reached 50 cents, a 40-cent change, or $24,000. For the fortunate buyer of oil at the lowest price, this meant a 40-fold increase, or 4,000% return on capital, for margins of $600. A subsequent drop from 50 cents to 15 cents gave a fearless short a profit opportunity of 35 cents, or over $20,000 in a year's period. Like the other two, soybean oil has experienced a number of good-size uptrends and downtrends since (but not on the order of the 1973–4 trends).

Soybean oil ranks 12th in uptrend rankings, with an average uptrend of .495, or 49.5% of price. This means an uptrend beginning at 20 cents would carry to approximately 30 cents on the average before starting a downtrend. Its ranking on downtrends is 14 of 25 commodities, with an average downtrend of .279. A downtrend starting at 30 cents per pound would fall to about 21.60 cents on the average before beginning to rise again.

THE FUNDAMENTALS

Soybeans as a crop came into importance during World War II. The U.S. government (with price supports) encouraged growing increased amounts to make itself sufficient in fats and oils. They are grown principally in the mid-America area, in the grain belt areas and to the south.

The amount of soybeans available for use depends on crop production for the year and carry-over from prior years surplus stocks. The carry-over has ranged considerably each year, because of the close balance between supply and demand for that year, which accounts for the sharp price trends.

The government price-support program has not exerted much influence on soybean prices in some time, due mostly to the fact that market prices have stayed well above the support price.

Demand is split between human needs for edible fats and oils and livestock needs for feed. It is increasing steadily with the upward change in population, both human and livestock. Except for huge changes in supply, however, demand amount is relatively insensitive to price. Exports form a large part of the human side of the equation, however, and have been increasing over the years to claim more than 30% of the total demand. Food for Peace, Public Law 480 purchases, and other government export programs are part of exports, but Russian purchases, European increases, and Asian imports have been increasing and are the main ingredient in exports. Thus, Russian weather becomes an important influence. Also, production in other countries, principally Brazil and other South American countries, affects total supplies and U.S. prices dramatically. Anchovy production in Peru greatly affects soybean meal prices.

Supply is dependent on weather and planting intentions. Farmers decide by late winter how much acreage will be set aside for soybean production, and from there on crop period weather, from May to September, is the principal determinant of the crop size. Drought can sharply reduce crop yields, along with too moist weather.

IMPORTANT EVENTS TO LOOK FOR – AND THEIR EFFECTS

1. *Weekly Grain Market News* (USDA). Weekly issue detailing CCC sales, stocks, exports, all crop estimates, crop-loan data, domestic consumption, and export data.
2. *Fats and Oils Situation Reports* (USDA). Published five times a year, usually starting in January, April, June, September, and November. General economic conditions on soybean yield, disappearance (crushing and exports), processors margins, government programs.
3. *Feed Situation Report* (USDA). Five times a year issuance, starting right after the fats and oils report. Similar to above, for soybean meal and oil.
4. *Crop Production Report* (USDA). Issued monthly on or about the tenth, this most important of reports gives planting intentions, acreage, and yield estimates as of the beginning of the month.
5. *Stocks of Grain in all Positions Report.* Released about the third week in each month, shows stocks as of the first of the month.

THE RECORD: 1980–1

Parameters for the moving-average method applied to soybeans, soybean meal, and soybean oil are listed in Table 3, Chapter Four. Both years tested were good trended ones. The moving average performed well on all three commodities, and spectacularly in some.

Soybean net gains for 1980 amounted to over $1.00 per bushel, or over $5,000, and for an average margin of 30 cents, or $1,500, meant a return on capital of more than 300%. In 1981, the returns were even better. Profits accumulated to nearly $3 per bushel, or $15,000 per contract, meaning almost 1,000% return on capital put up.

Soybean meal trades netted $22 in 1980, or $2,200, and more than 200% on $1,000 margin requirements. Nineteen eighty-one results were really great — over $100 per ton, or $10,000 profit on each contract. Again, about a 1,000% return on margin monies, or capital.

Soybean oil has shown only modest profits, keeping with its ranking in uptrends and downtrend move sizes. In 1980, it netted about 350 points, or over $2,000, on $600 margin requirements, for a net return of 300%, plus. The results for 1981 were not quite so good, totaling only a little over 100 points, or $600, a modest 100% return.

(Refer to Table 19 for details of trades results for soybeans, soybean meal, and soybean oil.)

Table 19.

MOVING AVERAGE METHOD

CONTRACT PARAMETERS	POS	DATE IN	PRICE IN	DATE OUT	PRICE OUT	GAIN(LOSS)	MAX LOSS	OPEN DATE
SOYBEANS MAY 1980								
A P .100 .050								
	+1	61179	805.00	62979	764.00	−41.00	41.0	62979
	−1	62979	764.00	52080	612.00	+152.00	59.0	70979
	TOTAL					+111.00		
	AVE.GAIN 152.0 AVE.LOSS 41.0							
	RATIO G/L 3.7 SUCCESS RATE 0.50 NO. TRADES 2							
MAY 1981								
A P .100 .050								
	+1	63080	750.00	120580	909.50	+159.50	6.0	70180
	−1	120580	909.50	43081	778.50	+131.00	8.5	120880
	TOTAL					+290.50		
	AVE.GAIN 145.2 AVE.LOSS 0.0							
	RATIO G/L 0.0 SUCCESS RATE 1.00 NO. TRADES 2							

Table 19. (Continued)

MOVING AVERAGE METHOD

CONTRACT PARAMETERS	POS	DATE IN	PRICE IN	DATE OUT	PRICE OUT	GAIN(LOSS)	MAX LOSS	OPEN DATE
SOYBEAN MEAL								
MAY 1980								
A P								
.100 .050								
	+1	60879	214.50	62979	202.50	−12.00	12.5	62979
	−1	62979	202.50	52080	168.00	+34.50	18.5	70979
	TOTAL					+22.50		
	AVE.GAIN	34.5 AVE.LOSS	12.0					
	RATIO G/L	2.8 SUCCESS RATE	0.50 NO. TRADES	2				

MAY 1981								
A P								
.100 .050								
	+1	70280	212.80	120380	271.30	+58.50	3.3	70380
	−1	120380	271.30	43081	226.90	+44.40	5.2	120480
	TOTAL					+102.90		
	AVE.GAIN	51.4 AVE.LOSS	0.0					
	RATIO G/L	0.0 SUCCESS RATE	1.00 NO. TRADES	2				

MOVING AVERAGE METHOD

CONTRACT PARAMETERS	POS	DATE IN	PRICE IN	DATE OUT	PRICE OUT	GAIN(LOSS)	MAX LOSS	OPEN DATE
SOYBEAN OIL								
MAY 1980								
A B								
.100 .050								
	+1	61179	2755.00	73079	2597.00	−158.00	175.0	73079
	−1	73079	2597.00	52080	2090.00	+507.00	228.0	91879
	TOTAL					+349.00		
	AVE.GAIN	507.0 AVE.LOSS	158.0					
	RATIO G/L	3.2 SUCCESS RATE	0.50 NO. TRADES	2				

MAY 1981								
A B								
.100 .050								
	+1	63080	2562.00	92680	2698.00	+136.00	17.0	70180
	−1	92680	2698.00	110580	2957.00	−259.00	262.0	110580
	+1	110580	2957.00	120580	2790.00	−167.00	211.0	120580
	−1	120580	2790.00	43081	2384.00	+406.00	10.0	120880
	TOTAL					+116.00		
	AVE.GAIN	271.0 AVE.LOSS	213.0					
	RATIO G/L	1.2 SUCCESS RATE	0.50 NO. TRADES	4				

IN THE FUTURE

Soybeans and its by-products relate readily to weather as the main determinant in price moves.   If the U.S. or USSR has bad weather, prices can and do explode upward.   Bumper crops, of course, drastically reduce prices.

Weather is not a function of politics or any other human endeavor, so I do not see any reason current and long-term price patterns, reflecting for the most part weather, will not repeat.   That is, a steady diet of strong uptrends and weak downtrends alternating, perhaps as often as every other year, and sometimes less frequently.

21.
Sugar Profits

World sugar is traded on the New York Coffee and Sugar Exchange. The contract calls for 50 long tons, or 112,000 pounds, and prices are quoted in cents per pound. A one-cent move is equivalent to $1,120, and 5 cents is equal to $5,600 on one contract. Trading volume has been consistently firm, averaging around 10,000 contracts per day. Large numbers of speculators and hedgers trade the contract.

THE PROFIT POTENTIAL

Sugar has had some very different price patterns in the past. Much of the time, in the 1950s and 1960s, prices were rather dormant and stayed in the 3–5 cent area. Recently, great imbalances in supply and demand (monthly scarcity or *perceived* lack of supply) have created great run-ups of price at least three times in the past twenty years. (See Figure 40 for a price graph of sugar.)

The first one, in 1963, ran up from 3 cents to 13 cents, a 10-cent, or $11,200, move on margin requirements of $300, or return on capital of 3,700%. A downtrend of the same magnitude followed shortly.

The next big move did not occur until 1974, when inflation and a shortage hit the market. Prices rose from 10 cents to 65 cents, the huge, all-time largest move to date. The move amounted to 55 cents in less than one year, or over $60,000. On average margins of around $1,000, this equates to a whopping 6,000% return on capital. Finally, an uptrend move from around 8 cents to over 45 cents from 1979–81

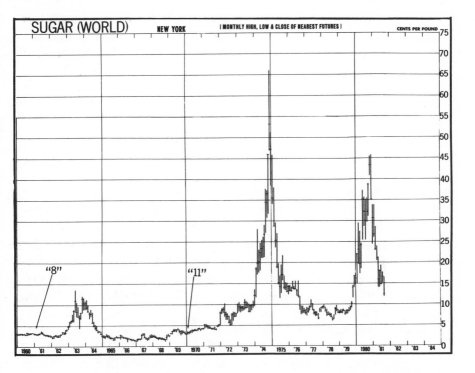

Figure 40. Sugar #11—monthly chart. (Courtesy of Commodity Research Bureau, Inc., New York, N.Y.)

returned 37 cents, or over $40,000 on invested capital. Downtrends of similar proportions and lengths of time occurred right after the respective uptrends.

Sugar has great propensity, vis-à-vis the foregoing examples, to retrace its uptrends and return completely to its starting price. This is due to the overbuying of sugar, the quick and huge imbalance (or perception of such; it is not always true), and the equally large realization that new supplies will quickly remedy the imbalance. The large trends and reactions make for ideal use of trend-following methods. (Refer to *The Record: 1980–1* for dramatic examples of large profits.)

Sugar ranks very high in uptrend price move averages, fourth, and just behind silver. Its average move is .684, which means that an uptrend starting at 20 cents will, on the average, move to 33.70 before topping out and starting a downtrend.

It also ranks well in downtrends. Right behind soybean meal, it ranks 7th of 25 commodities with an average downtrend move size of .320. A downtrend starting at 30 cents would fall to 20.40 cents before bottoming and proceeding upwards, on the average.

THE FUNDAMENTALS

To many countries in the world and in times past (over one hundred years ago), sugar was king of commerce. Today, controls within colonial and internal quotas keep a large chunk of sugar supplies at relatively fixed prices. The free sugar mark accounts for about a third of total world supply and is known as world sugar, which is the commodity traded on the New York Coffee and Sugar Exchange.

Sugar is affected by many factors, one of which is the level of income in underdeveloped and emerging nations. There, sugar is considered a luxury and quantities consumed depend much on price levels, whereas in developed countries like the U.S., demand is inelastic to price.

Sugar stocks at the beginning of the sugar year (September 1) are a major determinant of whether prices will swing widely or not the following year. Weather takes over as the main influencing factor from then on. Cane and beets, the principal sources of sugar, are susceptible at least to insects and to disease.

Other demand factors also influence price. International tensions and conflicts, drastic changes in international trade patterns (Cuba radically changed its export arrangements and potential and growing capability when Castro took over the country in 1959), and currency stability.

IMPORTANT EVENTS TO LOOK FOR –
AND THEIR EFFECTS

1. *Sugar Reports* (USDA). Market reviews, world and U.S. statistics are presented monthly.
2. *F.O. Licht's International Sugar Report.* One of the best reports, it covers daily and bimonthly statistics on the world economy.
3. *Crop Production* (USDA). Monthly report contains estimates on beet and cane production.

THE RECORD: 1980-1

Parameters for the moving-average method applied to sugar are listed in Table 3, Chapter Four. Both years tested were very trended, both up and down, and the trading results reflect this feature. (Refer to Table 20 for details on the trading.)

In 1980, net gains amounted to about 15 cents, or $16,000 on margins in the $2,000 area, or a return on capital of about 800%.

Even better results were recorded in 1981. Two trends, one uptrend and one downtrend, gave the fortunate trader over 22 cents net profit, or nearly $25,000, a move of ten-fold, or 1,000% return on his margin.

Table 20.

MOVING AVERAGE METHOD

CONTRACT PARAMETERS	POS	DATE IN	PRICE IN	DATE OUT	PRICE OUT	GAIN(LOSS)	MAX LOSS	OPEN DATE
SUGAR#11								
MAY 1980								
A P								
.100 .050								
	+1	70579	1076.00	30780	2274.00	+1198.00	72.0	72479
	-1	30780	2274.00	41080	2188.00	+86.00	0.0	30780
	+1	41080	2188.00	43080	2419.00	+231.00	13.0	41480
TOTAL						+1515.00		
AVE.GAIN 505.0 AVE.LOSS 0.0								
RATIO G/L 0.0 SUCCESS RATE 1.00 NO. TRADES 3								
MAY 1981								
A P								
.100 .050								
	+1	41080	2470.00	70780	3389.00	+919.00	0.0	41080
	-1	70780	3389.00	80480	3407.00	-18.00	76.0	70880
	+1	80430	3407.00	82580	3207.00	-200.00	217.0	82580
	-1	82580	3207.00	91180	3639.00	-432.00	432.0	91180
	+1	91180	3639.00	111380	3946.00	+307.00	0.0	91130
	-1	111380	3946.00	10581	3327.00	+619.00	99.0	112080
	+1	10581	3327.00	11281	3002.00	-325.00	337.0	11281
	-1	11281	3002.00	43081	1600.00	+1402.00	73.0	11481
TOTAL						+2272.00		
AVE.GAIN 811.7 AVE.LOSS 243.7								
RATIO G/L 3.3 SUCCESS RATE 0.50 NO. TRADES 8								

IN THE FUTURE

Sugar has become very active in recent years, due to international crises and lack of much carry-over stocks, or inventory, to fill expanding demand due in part to increasing consumption by underdeveloped nations gaining more affluence.

I expect more trends of the same, with the net price move, or long, long term trend, to be upward over the years. This is an excellent vehicle for trend-following methods to make money.

22.
Wheat Profits

Wheat is traded on several North American exchanges, but the most heavily traded one is the Chicago Board of Trade. A contract consists of 5,000 bushels of wheat. A one-cent price move equals $50, and a 50-cent move means $2,500. Wheat is one of the most heavily traded commodities, and has a long history going back to the beginnings of the exchange in the days following the Civil War. Trading volume currently stands in the 20,000-plus category. Large numbers of hedgers and speculators divide trading interest, with hedging interest still quite dominant.

THE PROFIT POTENTIAL

Wheat has had a long, beribboned history — through wars, depressions, good economic times, and lulls. In recent times, it has gone through two stages — the low-priced and little-variation price movements of the 1950s and 1960s, and the current phase, high prices and large price swings.

The biggest uptrend occurred in 1972, when (unbeknown to the American farmer, government officials, and the public, but known to a few exporters) Russia purchased huge quantities of wheat because of crop failure. The resultant price eruption, starting at $1.50 per bushel, lasted into 1974 before subsiding from a peak of about $6.50. The length of the move, $5.00, was approximately fifty times the margin required to take a position: return on capital amounted to 5,000%. (See Figure 41 for a graph of wheat prices.)

Figure 41. Wheat—monthly prices. (Courtesy of Commodity Research Bureau, Inc., New York, N.Y.)

There have been several other uptrends since (1974, 1975, 1977), all trying to top the price of the first move, but having failed. The last one has lasted three years, and spanned over $3.00 in move, from $2.25 to $5.25. With an average margin of around 20 cents, the total return amounted to 1,500%.

Three major downtrends have also occurred. The largest occurred right after the longest uptrend, in 1974. Prices fell from the peak at $6.50 to below $3.50, a move of $3.00 in just a few months. The other downtrends amounted to $2.00 and $2.50 per bushel.

Wheat has ranked only in the middle of the uptrend rankings, 15th of the 25 commodities ranked. Its uptrend average size of .444 means that an uptrend starting at $4.00 would top out at $5.78 on the average before beginning a downtrend.

It shows up even more mediocre in downtrends. Wheat ranks 20th of 25, with an average downtrend move size of .244. A downswing in prices from the $5.00 level would bottom out at $3.78 before beginning an uptrend. With a margin of 30 cents currently, this does not give the trader too much room to maneuver with his timing method to make money.

THE FUNDAMENTALS

Wheat is harvested around the world in almost every month of the year, and in many parts of the world, including Australia, China, Europe, South America, and North America.

American supply and pricing is influenced by two main factors: government actions and weather. Some government programs affect plantings, such as price support, loans, and diversions payments; and others affect exports, such as Public Law 480. Availability of commercial storage, transportation, and shipping are important short-run determinants of supply. Weather affects the size of the crop — too little snow cover or drought can drastically reduce the yield, and too much rain can wash away seed or degrade the quality of the wheat.

Exports and domestic usage make up the sources for wheat demand. Government exports, such as Food for Peace, are made under Public Law 480, and commercial exports, which constitute the great bulk of demand, are made to countries around the world, principally Russia, Eastern European nations, Japan, Western Europe, China, India, and some Mideast countries. The amount exported is heavily dependent on world crop conditions and, hence, on weather around the world.

Domestic usage consists of food, feed, seed, individual feed, and military requirements. Wheat is sometimes fed to livestock when other feed becomes expensive relative to wheat.

Seed usage constitutes about 5 to 10 percent of domestic usage. Food consumption is by far the largest single use, and varies little from year to year because it reflects per capita consumption and (primarily) number of consumers, or population.

Wheat prices have a seasonal tendency to become low at harvest time in the fall, when supplies are heavy, and to rise to a high after December, some time in the May to July period.

IMPORTANT EVENTS TO LOOK FOR –
AND THEIR EFFECTS

1. *Crop Production Report* (USDA).   Monthly all-important estimates on planting intentions (late winter), acreage, yield, and crop size.   Conrad Leslie's Report, a private service, usually precedes it by a few days.
2. *Wheat Situations Report* (USDA). Four times a year (March, May, August, and November), subjects cover recent developments, government programs, current outlook, prospects for the next year, and the world situation.
3. *Grain Market News* (USDA). Weekly reporting on activities of government programs (particularly P.L. 480) and exports of wheat and flour, supply and disposition monthly, storage capacity of elevators and warehouses, monthly exports, and Canadian acreage estimates.
4. *Quarterly Stock of Grains in All Positions Report* (USDA). Issued about the 24th of each month, it provides information on stocks of wheat by size, location, and ownership, as of January 1, April 1, July 1, and October 1.

THE RECORD: 1980–1

Parameters for the moving-average method applied to wheat are listed in Table 3, Chapter Four. The two years tested were quite turbulent. In 1980, trends vacillated often between $4.10 and $4.65, a tight range, while it moved about $1.00 per bushel in 1981.

Trading results reflected the market conditions very closely. Net losses amounted to almost 80 cents, or $4,000, in 1980, while gains were only about 30 cents in 1981. See Table 20 for details of the trading.

Stops would have helped a lot for wheat. Fifteen-cents stops in 1980 would have reduced losses to about 40 cents, while increasing gains in 1981 to about 80 cents – almost a reverse of the results with no stops.

Table 20.

MOVING AVERAGE METHOD

CONTRACT PARAMETERS		POS	DATE IN	PRICE IN	DATE OUT	PRICE OUT	GAIN (LOSS)	MAX LOSS	OPEN DATE
WHEAT (CHI)									
MAY 1980									
A	P								
.100	.030								
		+1	50279	381.50	72379	443.00	+61.50	10.5	50879
		−1	72379	443.00	81479	449.00	−6.00	6.0	81479
		+1	81479	449.00	90679	439.75	−9.25	18.5	90579
		−1	90679	439.75	91379	465.00	−25.25	26.7	91379
		+1	91379	465.00	102679	442.25	−22.75	22.7	102679
		−1	102679	442.25	111479	467.25	−25.00	27.2	111479
		+1	111479	467.25	10980	435.75	−31.50	31.5	10980
		−1	10980	435.75	11780	462.50	−26.75	28.2	11780
		+1	11780	462.50	31080	439.00	−23.50	28.0	31080
		−1	31080	439.00	50580	412.00	+27.00	4.0	31180
		+1	50580	412.00	52080	414.00	+2.00	8.0	51280

TOTAL   −79.50
AVE.GAIN   30.1 AVE.LOSS   21.2
RATIO G/L   1.4 SUCCESS RATE 0.27 NO. TRADES 11

MAY 1981									
A	P								
.100	.030								
		+1	40380	467.50	41880	443.00	−24.50	26.5	41880
		−1	41880	443.00	50580	477.00	−34.00	34.0	50580
		+1	50580	477.00	60280	446.50	−30.50	30.5	60280
		−1	60280	446.50	62380	476.50	−30.00	31.5	62380
		+1	62380	476.50	120380	528.75	+52.25	14.0	72180
		−1	120380	528.75	43081	433.75	+95.00	4.2	120480

TOTAL   +28.25
AVE.GAIN   73.6 AVE.LOSS   29.7
RATIO G/L   2.4 SUCCESS RATE 0.33 NO. TRADES 6

IN THE FUTURE

Wheat should dramatically surge upward periodically (every two years) due to increased foreign demand (bad weather and crops) and inflation. The best trading should be on the long side, where the method works best.

Additional Readings

Casey, Douglas. *Crisis Investing.* New York: Harper and Row, 1979.

English, J. W., and Gray, Emerson Cardiff. *The Coming Real Estate Crash.* New Rochelle, N.Y.: Arlington House, 1979.

Barnes, Robert M. *Taming the Pits: A Technical Approach to Commodity Trading.* New York: John Wiley & Sons, 1979.

Smith, Jerome. *The Coming Currency Collapse.* New York: Books in Focus, 1980.

Tewles, Richard J., Harlow, Charles U., Stone, Herbert L. *The Commodity Futures Game: Who Wins? Who Loses? Why?* New York: McGraw-Hill, 1974.

Index

Catastrophe, 2
Cattle
    events, important, 77
    fundamentals, 76-77
    profit potential, 74-76
    trading record, 77-79
Cocoa
    events, important, 82-83
    fundamentals, 81
    profit potential, 80-81
    trading record, 83-84
Coffee
    events, important, 88
    fundamentals, 87-88
    profit potential, 85-87
    trading record, 88-89
Copper
    events, important, 92
    fundamentals, 92
    profit potential, 90-91
    trading record, 93-94
Commodity futures
    facts, 31-46
    history, 25-26
    investment medium, 22-24
    mechanics, 29-31
    need for, 26-29
    operation, 24-50
    orders, 46-47
    profit potential, 21
    statements, 47-49
    taxes, 49-50

Corn
    events, important, 98
    fundamentals, 97-98
    profit potential, 95-97
    trading record, 98-99
Cotton
    events, important, 103
    fundamentals, 102-103
    profit potential, 100-102
    trading record, 103-104
Currencies
    events, important, 111-112
    fundamentals, 111
    profit potential, 106-111
    trading record, 112-118

Depression
    forms of, 9-10
    four relationships, 3-5
Dow Jones Industrial Average, 2

Factor, penetration, 60-61
Financial instruments
    events, important, 124
    fundamentals, 122-124
    profit potential, 119-122
    trading record, 124-128

Gold
    events, important, 132
    fundamentals, 131-132
    profit potential, 129-131

Gold (cont.)
  trading record, 132-133

Hogs
  events, important, 136
  fundamentals, 135-136
  profit potential, 134-135
  trading record, 137-138

Index
  business production, 3-4
  wholesale price, 2-4
Inflation, super, causes of, 5-9
Investments
  management plan, 51–70
    formula plan, 64–70
    special situation, 62–64
  rainbow of, 13–16

Lumber
  events, important, 141
  fundamentals, 140-141
  profit potential, 139-140
  trading record, 142-143

Moving averages, 55-60

Orange juice
  events, important, 146
  fundamentals, 146
  profit potential, 144-146
  trading record, 146-148

Pork bellies
  events, important, 151-152

Pork bellies (cont.)
  fundamentals, 151
  profit potential, 149-151
  trading record, 152-153
Profit
  finder, 52-54
  timer, 55-62

Reward-risk, relationships, 16-19

Silver
  events, important, 156
  fundamentals, 156
  profit potential, 154-156
  trading record, 157-158
Soybean complex
  events, important, 164
  fundamentals, 163-164
  profit potential, 159-163
  trading record, 164-167
Stop range, 61-62
Sugar
  events, important, 170
  fundamentals, 170
  profit potential, 168-170
  trading record, 171-172

Trading results, explanations, 71-73

Wheat
  events, important, 176
  fundamentals, 175
  profit potential, 173-175
  trading record, 176-177